ॐ JACQUELINE BERNARD

Journey Toward Freedom

The Story of Sojourner Truth

Introduction by Nell Irvin Painter

The Feminist Press at The City University of New York
NEW YORK

Published in 1990 by the Feminist Press at the City University of New York,
The Graduate Center, 365 Fifth Avenue, Suite 5406, New York, NY 10016 /
www.feministpress.org

07 06 05 04 03 02   7 6 5 4

Library of Congress Cataloging-in-Publication Data

Bernard, Jacqueline.
  Journey toward freedom: the story of Sojourner Truth / by
Jacqueline Bernard; introduction by Nell Irvin Painter.
    p. cm.
  Reprint. Originally published: New York: Norton, 1967.
  Includes bibliographical references.
  Summary: A biography of Sojourner Truth, who was born into
slavery, freed in 1827, and became famous for her courage, quick
wit, and ready challenge as she campaigned for abolition and
women's rights in New York and the Midwestern States.
    ISBN 1-55861-023-5: $29.95 — ISBN 1-55861-024-3 (pbk.): $10.95
    1. Truth, Sojourner, d. 1883. 2. Afro-Americans—Biography.
3. Abolitionists—United States—Biography. 4. Social reformers—
United States—Biography. 5. Abolitionists. [1. Truth, Sojourner,
d. 1883. 2. Afro-Americans—Biography. 3. Reformers.]   I. Title.
E185.97.T8B47   1990
305.5'67'092—dc20
[B]
[92]   90-34481
                                                               CIP
                                                                AC

This publication is made possible, in part, by public funds from the
New York State Council on the Arts. The Feminist Press is also grateful to Nida E. Thomas and Caroline Urvater for their generosity.

Cover design: Ife Nii Owoo
Cover photograph courtesy of the Burton Historical Collection of
the Detroit Public Library

*This edition is dedicated to the mother and
granddaughters of Jacqueline Bernard:
Louise Paine de Sieyes, Eliza Jacqueline Hunter Bernard,
and Susannah Louise Hunter Bernard.*

Contents

Author's Note

An anthology of Negro writings that I chanced to pick up while a student at the University of Chicago brought me my first glimpse of Sojourner Truth. Although history was my field, this was also my first inkling that Negroes had made any contribution to American history beyond the well-known fact of their slave labor. Sojourner's powerful personality, her strong-minded opinions and no-nonsense behavior—as well as the very practical inspiration she brought to her struggle for her people's rights—made me suspect I had been missing a great deal. I also suspected I had only glimpsed the top of a hidden iceberg. There must be other fighters in American history like this. My "good education" clearly had left some yawning gaps.

At that time, I conceived the vague idea that I would "some day" write a book for young people and try to make sure that they had a chance to hear something about this kind of American woman.

But only many years later, when I started to pursue the research for my book, did I really discover Sojourner Truth. I had expected to find a young rebel. Instead I found a frightened, lonely slave child, torn from her family, beaten by new masters. Later, as a young woman, she had for many years been the hardworking, obedient slave of a master whose sole claim to her gratitude was that he was reasonably kind.

Only very slowly, through the stubborn personal effort that characterized all her struggles, did Sojourner teach herself to separate truth from the falsehoods around her. In that struggle, she found her courage and her freedom, and with these the strength to help free others. Today, many young and old Americans are waging a similar personal struggle—and continuing her journey toward freedom for all Americans.

This is the story of Sojourner Truth as I understand it. In telling it, wherever possible, I have used actual conversations as originally spoken and recorded in the primary sources listed in the first paragraph of the bibliography on page 255.

Jacqueline Bernard

Acknowledgments

For their generous assistance in researching this book, I owe major thanks to the staffs of the New York Historical Society, and the American History Room and the Schomburg Collection of the New York Public Library. I would also like to acknowledge the helpfulness of the following collections and their staffs: the Long Island Historical Society, the Museum of the City of New York, the Sophia Smith Collection of the Smith College Library, the Slavery and Abolition Collection of the Cornell University Library, the New York State Historical Association, the Rochester Historical Society, the Senate House Museum in Kingston, the Division of Archives and History and the New York State Library of the State University, the Gerrit Smith Collection of the Syracuse University Library, the Antislavery Collection of the Boston Public Library, and the Columbia Historical Society in Washington, D.C.

In addition, I would like to offer my particular thanks to Mrs. Ruth P. Heidgerd of New Paltz and Miss Agnes Scott Smith of Kingston, whose interest in and knowledge of Ulster County, and whose willingness to give their time, saved me days of uncertain research.

J.B.

List of Illustrations

Introduction

Nell Irvin Painter

Sojourner Truth's memory is a study in the power of words. To start with, her very name commands attention: someone named "Sojourner Truth" must have been somebody. Second, the pithy comments that made her enduring reputation sum up wisdom that every right-thinking person recognizes as true, long before having put the truth into words. In the nineteenth and early twentieth centuries her best-known phrase was "Frederick, is God dead?" Today we are more likely to associate her with another rhetorical question: "Ar'n't I a woman?"

The reputations of Sojourner Truth and Harriet Tubman, also a former slave who was active in the mid-nineteenth century, have somehow survived several generations. But unlike

Tubman, who led hundreds of slaves to freedom and is remembered, appropriately, as the "Moses of her people," Truth's ac-
tions are not so easily characterized. Few who know her name
can recall what, exactly, she is famous for beyond her lines.
This very mystery creates a curiosity about the person behind
the phrases and draws readers to life-writing about her,
whether in the form of biography or autobiography.

SOJOURNER TRUTH LIFE-WRITING

Throughout her life Sojourner Truth (c. 1797–1883) was il-
literate, which means that virtually everything we know of her
comes either through other people's documentation or information she narrated to others.[1] Her first piece of life-writing,
The Narrative of Sojourner Truth, which she published herself
with the assistance of a Connecticut abolitionist amanuensis
named Olive Gilbert, appeared in 1850. This third-person
biography is very much an as-told-to story that includes
Gilbert's interpretations of what she thought Truth must have
been feeling at given times. It consists of a 128-page narrative
that covers her life through slavery, emancipation in 1827, and
activities as a freedwoman up to 1849. Later editions of *The
Narrative of Sojourner Truth,* which appeared in 1878 and
1885, added reprints of newspaper clippings and quotations
from Truth's "Book of Life," which was essentially an autograph book in which she collected greetings and signatures of
famous people, including President Abraham Lincoln. The *Narrative* forms the bases of all subsequent biographical writing
about Truth. Harriet Beecher Stowe drew upon it to prepare
the most widely circulated nineteenth-century essay on Truth,
"Sojourner Truth, the Libyan Sibyl," which appeared in the
April 1863 issue of the *Atlantic Monthly.*
    In the late nineteenth and early twentieth centuries, Truth's
memory remained alive thanks to new editions of her *Narrative*
and short entries in anthologies and collected biographies. The
first volume of *The History of Woman Suffrage* (1881) includes
the "Reminiscences" by Frances D. Gage, which had also ap-

peared in the 1878 edition of Sojourner Truth's *Narrative*. Gage's account presents the most familiar version of what has come to be known as the "Ar'n't I a Woman?" speech of 1851. In 1902 Pauline Hopkins, editor of *The Colored American*, published a short biographical sketch of Truth in her magazine.[2]

The first full-length biography of Truth, *God's Faithful Pilgrim*, by Arthur Huff Fauset, an anthropology professor at Howard University, appeared in 1937. The book was the first volume of what was to have been a series of biographies of prominent African Americans.[3] Thanks to Fauset's book and to short entries in collective biographies, Truth remained firmly implanted in African-American historiography until the Civil Rights era, which produced two new full-length biographies.

Interestingly enough, both of Truth's 1960s biographers were Left-leaning women of European heritage. Hertha Pauli, originally from Austria, published *Her Name Was Sojourner Truth* in 1962.[4] Five years later, Jacqueline Bernard, originally from France, published *Journey Toward Freedom*, republished for the first time in this edition. Neither Fauset, Pauli, or Bernard was a professional historian, and all three wrote for general and young readers, aiming, perhaps, for their most likely audiences and recognizing, certainly, the difficulty of presenting any kind of rigorously historical biography of a subject who lacked personal papers entirely.

JOURNEY TOWARD FREEDOM

First published in 1967, Jacqueline Bernard's *Journey Toward Freedom* received prominent and positive reviews. Robert Coles reviewed the book in the Washington *Post*, and Richard Elman, in the *New York Times Book Review*, remarked that Bernard was "quietly factual" in her presentation of history and "lyrical when the demand arises." The *Times Book Revew* listed *Journey Toward Freedom* as one of the best books of 1967. The *Saturday Review* found the biography "inspiring."[5]

Using material from *The Narrative of Sojourner Truth*, Stowe's "Libyan Sibyl," and a variety of local and specialized histories, Bernard constructed the backbone of her biography of Truth. To appeal to general readers, she added dialogue, some from the *Narrative*, other from her own imagination. *Journey Toward Freedom* is a narrative history that closely follows its sources, giving a whole chapter to Sojourner Truth's encounter with roughnecks one evening in the woods of western Massachusetts and a chapter to Truth's residence in the Northampton Association in 1844–1846, which brought her into contact with Garrisonian abolitionists and women's rights advocates. While Truth's ability to calm young men who had intended initially to disrupt her camp meeting demonstrates her powers of persuasion, the episode does not represent a turning point in Truth's development. However, the importance of Truth's stay in Northampton cannot be understated, as it remade her public persona. Having been an itinerant preacher along Methodist and Millerite lines since she had taken the name Sojourner Truth in 1843, after Northampton Truth began to speak up for anti-slavery and feminist causes. Without her stay at the Northampton Association, Sojourner Truth probably would not have become any better known than other black women preachers of the antebellum era such as her fellow Methodists, Jarena Lee and Zilpha Elaw.[6]

General readers may still read Bernard with satisfaction, for, despite a few historical inaccuracies, her story is sound. Her readers will learn when Isabella Van Wagenen became Sojourner Truth, what she did on the lecture circuit, and with whom she traveled. Bernard is particularly good on Truth's last years, during which she secured aid for the freedpeople and collected signatures on a petition to Congress for western lands.

Journey Toward Freedom does contain a few small errors. Contrary to Bernard's recountal, Isabella/Sojourner Truth had attended camp meetings before 1843 (p. 124). In fact, she had begun to make a reputation as a gifted preacher shortly after her arrival in New York City in 1829. The book is factually misleading in one instance only, the year in which Truth asked Frederick Douglass whether God were dead. Perhaps for rhetorical punch, Bernard puts this question into the same chapter with Truth's speech before the Akron women's rights convention of 1851, when she asked "and ar'n't I a woman?" (p. 167). Truth confronted Douglass in 1859, after Douglass and John Brown had held extensive conversations and Douglass was doubting whether the abolition of slavery could be accomplished peaceably.[7]

The most interesting aspects of Bernard's interpretation of Sojourner Truth concern Truth's feelings about race. In this regard Bernard takes two approaches. She emphasizes material that is mentioned in passing in the *Narrative*, and she makes up scenes that do not appear in the *Narrative* at all. In the first instance, Bernard presents an enslaved Isabella who is an intensely lonely young woman whose loneliness is her own doing. This Isabella has chosen to give her loyalty to her master, John Dumont, whom she identifies with God. Isabella takes great satisfaction—which Bernard characterizes as an "obsession"—in pleasing Dumont, for which her fellow slaves make fun of her. In two separate passages, Bernard quotes their taunting Isabella with the jeer: "White man's pet!" (In the *Narrative* Isabella says once that Dumont's slaves called her "white man's nigger.") Cut off from friendship and support from her fellow slaves by her attachment to Dumont, Bernard's Isabella nonetheless fails to forge close ties with whites. She misses the company of black people, realizing all the while that she is incapable of being truly close to her fellow slaves. In the early pages of *Journey Toward Freedom*, Isabella's feelings towards her fellow slaves are deeply ambivalent. Bernard writes that she was "a young woman alone in both the white and black worlds."[8]

According to both the *Narrative* and Bernard, Isabella had a brief love affair that ended tragically. Then Isabella married Tom, an older man who was also a slave of John Dumont's, evidently at Dumont's instigation. Although Isabella bore Tom five children , *Journey Toward Freedom* depicts an empty relationship between Tom and Isabella, as though Isabella felt no attachment to her husband. As sources that would illuminate these emotions do not exist, it is not possible to know whether her relationship with Tom was characterized by the same ambivalence that Bernard sees in the young Isabella's relationships with other black people, including Tom. But the *Narrative* seems to point toward a warmer union, a fairly ordinary, nineteenth-century, working-class marriage that was neither coercive nor middle-class-companionate. Isabella felt enough confidence in Tom to leave her children in his care when she went to New York City in 1829.

Bernard's Isabella/Sojourner Truth is a woman who loves her children intensely but who cannot afford to have them with her until she moves to Battle Creek, Michigan, in 1856. In Battle Creek, Truth gathers her daughters (she had lost contact with her only son, Peter, when he was a young sailor in the early 1830s) and grandchildren around her in a house that she pays for by lecturing and selling her book, songs, and calling cards. Yet even when she is surrounded by family and depends on them, Bernard's Truth remains a more solitary character than appears in the *Narrative*.

Bernard's most inventive interpretation relates to Isabella's discovery of Methodism in 1828. Bernard describes Isabella's witnessing of a service in a new Methodist church in her Ulster County neighborhood, in which members of the congregation tell how they found Jesus. As all those inside the church are white, Isabella does not enter. But she watches the service from outside for several hours. As Isabella realizes the similarity between her own conversion experience and those described by the Methodists, Bernard quotes her saying to herself: "How can white folks be so much like me?" (p. 87). On second reading, one realizes that "so much like me" means "having had religious experiences similar to mine." But given the portrayal of an Isabella suspended between two racial (not religious) worlds, the question seems at first to mean something both more literal and more general. It seems to say that Isabella, this lonely woman who had felt at home with neither white nor black people, found her community among whites. Creating an entire scene that does not occur in the *Narrative*, and having Isabella describe the congregants by race, Bernard emphasizes the whiteness over the Methodism of the beloved community that Isabella dicovers in 1828. This scene makes race more salient in *Journey Toward Freedom* than it is in the *Narrative*.

I suspect that Bernard realized the tenuousness of any attachment across racial lines in antebellum America and that she was saying (at least) two things at once in the quote in which Isabella realizes her identity with white Methodists. More obviously, Bernard lets Isabella find a group of people to whom she feels some ties. Yet by underlining the Methodists' race, Bernard warns readers that the identification between white Methodists and black Isabella cannot be complete or easy. The common religious identity that Isabella finds with white Methodists helps her leave Ulster County but does not give her an entirely new spiritual home. This description of Isabella's ambivalence and estrangement may apply equally well to Jacqueline Bernard's own experience.

JACQUELINE BERNARD

One of Bernard's friends observed that biographers do not choose their subjects haphazardly. Just as Bernard described Truth as "a powerful personality . . . [of] strong-minded opinions and no-nonsense behavior," so these phrases applied full well to Bernard herself. Bernard was unusually self-reliant, called by a playwright friend "one of the most sweetly independent women I have ever known." A person of great energy, Bernard was also a resourceful woman whose friends and acquaintances admired her spunk and good humor. One of her many friends remembered that "she always made you feel by her example that a woman on her own could lead a rich, full life." Yet she could also be self-righteous, judgmental, withdrawn, and ultimately mysterious. As readers come away from *Journey Toward Freedom* feeling that they cannot know Sojourner Truth fully, so friends sometimes felt that part of Jacqueline Bernard remained beyond their ken.[9]

Bernard lived an unusual life, all of which she did not reveal to the friends of her maturity. She was born Jacqueline de Sieyes in the French Alps in 1921; her father was a French count, her mother a Bostonian. The family left France when Jacqueline was a child, and she was raised in the United States. Although Bernard lived in Washington, D.C., with her mother, while her father lived in New York City, she felt closer to her father than to her mother. Graduating from the Madeira School in 1939, Bernard attended Vassar College for two years, during which she was a restless and mediocre student. By 1940 or 1941 she was casting about for adventure, pleading with her father to help her find work in a settlement house or join the Free French in Brazzaville in French Equatorial Africa. Failing in both ambitions, she dropped out of Vassar, spent a year at the University of Chicago, then made her way to Mexico City, where she worked on *Tiempo*, a weekly magazine, and met and married Allen Bernard. They had a son, Joel, in 1945. In 1949, they divorced. With another divorced friend, Bernard founded Parents Without Partners in 1956 but left the organization as it became little more than a place to meet people. "I was interested in social change, not a social life," she said.[10]

Between the end of her marriage and the publication of *Journey Toward Freedom*, Bernard worked at a variety of jobs that will sound familiar to educated women of her generation. She found employment as a waitress, factory worker, Macy's salesperson, substitute teacher, and in a host of other positions that were ill-paid and unchallenging. In the early 1960s, while her son was an undergraduate at Cornell University, she took courses at the City College of New York and began working on her biography of Sojourner Truth.

Without Bernard's testimony on the point, I cannot say exactly what drew her to Truth. A fellow writer and acquaintance, Dorothy Sterling, had mentioned the possibility of

Bernard's contributing a volume to a series of biographies for young people, but that project seems to have come to fruition as *Voices from the Southwest,* which Bernard published in 1973. The answer seems to lie in Bernard's personal politics. In the 1950s she was briefly a member of the Communist Party, which was the only political party in the United States at the time that put black civil rights at the top of its agenda. Although Bernard left the CP rather quickly—lacking, her son suspects, a sufficiently bureaucratic and sectarian personality for that organization at that time—she kept her concern for racial justice.[11] She began work on the Truth biography in 1962 and in 1964 raised money for northern students, including her son, who went to Mississippi to register black voters during Freedom Summer. In short, Bernard's biographical undertaking of the early 1960s did not represent a new turn in her thinking. Her sister recalls that Bernard had "*always* [been] interested in women of courage" and had long exhibited a "sensitivity to injustice. . . . Civil rights and racial equality had certainly been a central part of her thinking for a decade before [1962]."[12]

In the late 1960s, after W. W. Norton published *Journey Toward Freedom,* Bernard demonstrated against the Vietnam War and for the United Farm Workers. She published her book on Southwesterners and tried in vain to publish a similar book on Appalachian women. In 1969 Dell brought out a paperback edition of *Journey Toward Freedom,* but by the early 1970s both hardcover and softcover editions were out of print, despite having made bestseller lists with sales of more that 25,000 copies. As early as 1973 Bernard realized that Truth was becoming a heroine for feminists, and she wanted to revise *Journey Toward Freedom* so as to portray Truth as a feminist as well as an abolitionist. Bernard's Truth did not appear to be an attractive property to publishers in the 1970s and 1980s, so that neither Bernard nor her agent was able to get the book reprinted within her lifetime.

After going to dinner and attending a movie with friends, Jacqueline Bernard was murdered in her apartment on Riverside

Drive, New York, in August 1983. The murder has not been solved.

When I agreed to write this Introduction, I knew nothing about Jacqueline Bernard beyond the information conveyed in the paragraph at the back of the hardcover edition of *Journey Toward Freedom.* Having gotten to know her after her death, I feel doubly privileged to be able to comment on the lives of both an intriguing biographical subject and an engaging biographer. Both Truth and Bernard were fine, big, mature women with deep convictions about the value of every human life. Both were eloquent and fearless feminists who can teach us about women's strength and eloquence. Both had the knack of expressing their truths pungently, illuminating the worlds in which they lived. Both, finally, elude our complete understanding.

NOTES

I would like to thank Dorothy Sterling, Joel Bernard, Jean Fagan Yellin, Gerda Lerner, Susannah Driver, and Eva Moseley of the Schlesinger Library at Radcliffe College for their generous and invaluable assistance.

1. See Carleton Mabee, "Sojourner Truth, Bold Prophet: Why Did She Never Learn to Read?" *New York History* (January 1988), 55–77.

2. Elizabeth Cady Stanton, et al., eds. *History of Woman Suffrage,* vol. 1 (New York: Fowler & Wells, 1881), 115–117; Pauline Hopkins, *Colored American Magazine,* 1902.

3. Arthur Huff Fauset. *Sojourner Truth: God's Faithful Pilgrim* (Chapel Hill: University of North Carolina Press, 1938). The series did not continue.

4. Hertha Pauli. *Her Name Was Sojourner Truth* (New York: Appleton-Century-Crofts, 1962). The sister of the Nobel Prize physicist Wolfgang Pauli, Hertha Pauli had been an actress and playwright in Germany and in her native Vienna until the Nazi era. She moved to Paris after the Nazi occupation of Austria in 1938 and to the United States after the fall of France in 1940. In addition to her study of So-

journer Truth, Pauli also wrote a biography of Alfred Nobel, the inventor of dynamite. She died in New York in 1973, at the age of sixty-three.

5. *New York Times Book Review,* 26 Nov. 1967; *Saturday Review,* 16 Dec. 1967.

6. On Jarena Lee and Zilpha Elaw, see William Andrews, ed., *Sisters of the Spirit* (Bloomington, Ind.: University of Indiana Press, 1986).

7. Frederick Douglass, *The Life and Times of Frederick Douglass, Written by Himself* (New York, 1892), 275.

8. *Journey Toward Freedom,* 37–38, 40–42, 63.

9. Madelon Bedell, Eve Merriam, and Livia Turgeon, quoted in Linda Wolfe, "The Death of an Idealist: Who Killed Jacqui Bernard?" *New York Magazine,* 17 Oct. 1983, 67–68.

10. Quoted in Wolfe, 64.

11. Joel Bernard to Nell Irvin Painter, telephone interview, 14 Dec. 1989.

12. Henriette Montgomery to Dorothy Sterling, 21 Oct. 1988.

Journey Toward Freedom

The Story of Sojourner Truth

A Start in Life

ONE

&~ Sojourner Truth was born a slave in Ulster County, New York, some twenty-one years after the American Revolution. Ulster lies about eighty miles up the Hudson River from New York City. Gently rolling hills in its southern part rise in the north to the sharp granite peaks and irregular ridges of the Catskill and Shawangunk mountains. In Sojourner's childhood their slopes seemed dangerous and black, for in those days they were still covered with the dark hemlocks that had so frightened the superstitious early settlers and kept them from straying too far from the river.

Small brooks and twisting creeks trickled and tumbled through those hills, swelling the waters of the broad, slow-flowing Hudson. Sandburgh Creek, Rondout Creek, Platte Kill, Wall Kill—the creeks were named by the Dutch who had been the first to push up-river from their tiny Manhattan Island settlement, make peace with the Indians, and settle down to farm the fertile flats. They were industrious farmers. When Sojourner Truth was a child, it was said that you could tell a Dutchman's farm by the barn. The Dutch farmer spent his money on the barn while the Yankee would invest it in his house.

Sojourner's parents, Ma-Ma Betts and Bomefree, were owned by one of the many families of Dutch descent in the county. The day she was born, Colonel Johannes Hardenbergh stopped by just long enough to notice that his new possession was a healthy, long-limbed girl with shining blue-black skin. He nodded approvingly. "She'll make a sturdy worker," he said. Colonel Hardenbergh needed workers. He had one of the biggest farms in Ulster County.

The new baby was named Isabelle. But the slaves shortened the name to "Belle" while she was still a tiny round thing, sucking at her mother's breast or swinging in a basket from an apple tree branch outside the kitchen where Ma-Ma Betts worked. She never had a proper family name. As a slave she was not considered to "belong" to her mother or father. Like her parents, Belle belonged only to Colonel Hardenbergh. People outside would speak of her as "Colonel Hardenbergh's Belle" or sometimes simply as "Belle Hardenbergh." But Hardenbergh was not her own name; like the brand burned on a calf's side, the name merely announced the owner. A new master would mean a new name.

Sojourner never did know for sure when she was born. Not the year, the day of the month, nor even whether there was snow on the ground or dark summer leaves shading the oak branches.

No one ever recorded a slave's exact birth date. It had no importance to the owner, and slave parents had no way of knowing the calendar year, much less of writing it down. But Sojourner was probably born about 1797.

By that date, New York and New Jersey were the only northern states that still permitted slavery. Every other state north of Maryland and Delaware had abolished slavery soon after the American Revolution. Some had included an abolition clause in the original drafts of their state constitutions. But in New York and New Jersey, in large part because of these states' undemocratic land-owning systems, slavery was harder to abolish.

Early governors of New York had given huge tracts of land to their friends, who then built fine mansions and were known as patroons or lords of the manor. They were supposed to settle tenants on their land. But immigrants coming to America wanted to find a better life than the one they had left behind in feudal Europe; they wanted to own their own farms. Naturally they preferred to move to states where land was not under such a monopoly.

As a result, industry and agriculture developed slowly in New York. Big landowners like Colonel Hardenbergh never had enough workers and found slaves useful. But slaves were never as economical in the North as in the South, for the long winters prevented year-round labor. In New York, owning many slaves meant twelve to fifteen at the most. But like the southern plantation owner, the typical New York landowner enjoyed the aristocratic way of life made possible by black servants. And he enjoyed the political power he could wield as long as things remained as they were—like comfortable people anywhere, he was not keen to see things change.

Others felt different. The breakup of huge estates had started with the Revolution, when Tory property was seized and divided

among soldiers and tenant farmers. The more farsighted statesmen, too, wanted to see their state develop as it could do only
when its citizens were free to better themselves.

Among these statesmen were some who themselves owned
large estates and many slaves. John Jay was one. Jay, who later
became the first Chief Justice of the United States Supreme Court
and a governor of his state, struggled to have a clause abolish-
ing slavery inserted in the first state constitution in 1777. The
move was blocked. Yet even at that time, abolition failed by only
a very few votes. Thereafter, year after year, Jay drew up abolition
bills and presented them to the New York State Legislature.

The ideas for which men had fought the Revolution still tingled
in their minds. "To contend for liberty and to deny that blessing
to others involves an inconsistency not to be excused," wrote Jay.
Five thousand slaves had joined the struggle against the British,
and in return, they had been freed. Many of them had fought as
soldiers. Others had served as spies and wagoners, or had helped
to build fortifications. How much longer, many Americans asked,
could the brothers and sisters of such men be kept in chains? In
the end, practical reasons would decide, and, in New York, practical reasons were on the side of freedom.

Long before Belle was born, it was clear that slavery was
doomed in the state. In continuing to fight to retain his slaves,
even the big landowner knew he fought only a delaying action.
There were huge unexplored forests to open up in the western
part of the state, away from the more accessible Hudson Valley.
There were canals to dig. Scientific farming was needed. Yet men
who had the choice would not come to a state where big landowners hogged the land and slavery kept a workman's wages
down to a "small advance from nothing."

The long cold winters of New York State also helped weaken
the last resistance to abolition. There were certain advantages to

free labor that were plain even to the big landowner. A free man could be dismissed when there was no farm work to do, or if he grew too old or sick to be useful.

In 1785, abolitionists had persuaded the state legislature to forbid the bringing of additional slaves into the state for sale. Slaves living in New York were not to be sold out of state either. The man who violated these laws was forced to pay a 100-pound* fine, while his slave gained freedom.

By the same law, the manumission, or freeing, of slaves was made much easier. Previously, when a man freed even a strong, young slave he had to leave a sum of money with the town or manor for security to guard against the possibility that the slave, one day, might become a public charge. Even when the master granted his slave's freedom in his will, the slave was still dependent on the executor, or person who carried out the will, to provide security. Frequently the executor would refuse to pay the sum required, and no matter how hard the slave had worked to gain the freedom promised by his master, he had to remain in slavery.

The laws of 1785 softened this state of affairs: if the slave was less than fifty years old and able to provide for himself, his owner could free him simply by obtaining a certificate of manumission for him. No bond was needed. And even if the slave were over fifty and the owner failed to obtain the proper certificate, the slave still could be freed. But should such a slave require help later, the town legally could hold the owner responsible at that time for supporting him.

Quite a number of slave owners took advantage of the new law to free their slaves in their wills or to allow them to hire themselves out and earn money to buy their own freedom. Others, like certain Quakers who still owned slaves, for the first time found it

---

* The dollar did not come into general use in New York State until some years later.

possible to do what they had long believed was right without laying out large sums of money for security. Many of these manumitted all of their slaves during their own lifetimes.

The men who worried about the expense of feeding elderly slaves also favored the new law. By not bothering to obtain the manumission certificate, they could avoid laying out security for an old slave they wished to put out of the house. So many feeble old men and women were freed and left to fend for themselves in this way that it became a scandal. Another law was quickly passed, to strengthen the law that compelled a master to support his aged slaves, whether freed or not. Unfortunately, that law was poorly enforced. Travelers of the day have left many accounts of old men and women wandering helplessly around the Hudson Valley until they died of hunger and exposure.

If Isabelle had come into this changing and not very kindly world just two years later then she did, she would have been born "free," although the law would have required that she serve her master without pay until the age of twenty-five. A law to that effect was passed in 1799. Boys born after July 4 of that year were also born "free," but had to serve without pay until age twenty-eight.

Slavery was retreating under the new laws. But in 1797 there were still many slaves, especially among the Dutch farmers. Ulster County, with its many Dutch farmers, had more slaves than New York City itself. Ulster and the other Hudson counties formed the backbone of the resistance to abolition.

Belle's first master, the old Colonel, died when she was a baby, and Belle, her brother Peter, her parents, and the old man's ten other slaves all became the property of his son Charles. "We were lucky to go to Master Charles," her mother used to say. He was by far the best of the Hardenberghs.

Charles moved his new possessions to Hurley, where he had built a solid, comfortable house of limestone cut from the surrounding hills. In the master's quarters, big square rooms with

Belle was living in Ulster County when a local artist painted this view near the point where Rondout Creek empties into the Hudson River below Kingston.

broad plank floors looked out on trees and meadows sloping to a creek. But the room where the slaves slept was a long, narrow, damp cellar with only tiny slits of windows at the top of the steep wall. Those slits opened onto wells dug below ground level so that only an occasional beam of light could find its way in. The floor was of boards set loosely over the rough ground. At night the slaves spread straw across the boards to sleep on. Bodies stirring in sleep brought a slushy, sucking sound from mud and water underneath the boards.

The damp was especially hard on old people like Belle's father. His real name was James, but in his youth his height and straight back had earned him the nickname Bomefree or "tree" in the Low Dutch idiom spoken by most farmers of that area. According to Ma-Ma Betts, Bomefree had been a powerful worker. Belle remembered him only as an old man whose back was bent with rheumatism and whose stiff fingers swelled like knotholes at the knuckles.

Ma-Ma Betts was much younger than her husband. She was his third wife, the other two having been sold away from him. Belle remembered her mother as a lithe, tall woman, singing softly in a deep throaty voice as she moved about her work—strange, lovely songs to soothe a crying baby or to make work go faster. Ma-Ma said they were the songs sung by her mother, who came from a faraway land called Africa. Ma-Ma herself did not know what the words of the songs meant, but that made no difference.

At other times, Belle's mother would sit with her children under the stars and talk to them about a "Mighty Being," a "God who hears and sees you."

"Where does he live?" asked Belle.

"High in the sky," replied Ma-Ma, pointing straight toward the stars. "When you are beaten or cruelly treated or fall into any trouble, just ask him for help. He will always hear and help you." She made her children promise never to lie or steal but always to obey their master, and she taught them the words of the Lord's Prayer in Low Dutch, the only language any of them knew.

Belle and her younger brother Peter were Ma-Ma's only children at that time. There had been eleven others, but all had died or been sold away before Belle was old enough to notice.

Yet in later years it seemed as if she had known them all. For in the early winter evenings when it was too dark to work, her parents sometimes would relive for hours on end their last day with one or another lost child. Belle later particularly remembered sitting pressed against her mother's knee, staring into the flickering yellow flame of the pine knots that lit the cellar, until she seemed to see there the faces of the two children her parents spoke about the most.

The boy had been five and the girl only three on the freezing winter morning that they had been taken away by a man in a bright-red sleigh. Ma-Ma and Bomefree never tired of telling the story, nor Belle of hearing them describe how the boy had sat up "straight as a jack rabbit" on the front seat of the sleigh, not seeming to know why his master had put him there. Ma-Ma would insist he must have thought it was just for a ride. The master had come out a second time, now carrying the boy's baby sister. When he had closed the lid of the sleigh box gently but firmly over the head of the little girl, the boy had understood. Leaping from his seat, he had shot through the house like a partridge flushed by a hound. The master had quickly found him, hiding behind the woodpile, and had lifted him back into the sleigh. The sleigh had moved away—red and silver against the white snow.

Staring into the flames, Belle could see that sleigh moving away . . . moving away . . . moving away. . . .

Every time Ma-Ma told the story, she would moan and clench her hands at the memory and sob, "But my boy never run to me. He never run to me a single time when he was trying so hard to hide. He knew it was no use. His mama couldn't protect her own child."

Later, sighing, she would always add, "I tell you, I knew trouble was coming that day, from the first moment I woke up. As plain as your face looking at me now, Belle, black dispatch said to me that morning, 'Ma-Ma Betts, trouble is coming.'"

Belle knew all about "black dispatch." Slaves often seemed to get wind of things long before they happened. They would explain this intuitive knowledge by saying, "Black dispatch told me."

Sometimes, while thinking about all this, Belle felt troubled. Why hadn't Ma-Ma run away with her children when she received the warning? Belle had heard many stories of such flights. Several years before Hardenbergh's Joe had disappeared with three of his children. Master had sold the mother, and Joe was taking no chances. It was rumored that all four of them were living with the Indians, way up in the hills.

"Perhaps," Belle thought, "Ma-Ma didn't want to leave Bomefree. He's too old to go into the hills."

But Ma-Ma, in her own way, never stopped protesting against the slave owner. No matter how many children were torn from her, Ma-Ma continued to see herself as the mother of a very large family, struggling to hold her scattered children together.

"Belle, Peter, look!" she called out excitedly one night. Their faces tipped up, the children saw stars strewn across the sky as plump and thick as golden grains of Ulster County wheat pouring from a basket. "Right this minute," said Ma-Ma, "those same stars you see are shining down on all your brothers and sisters. No matter where they are, they see those stars as plain as you."

It was about this time that a rumor swept through the slave cellar, a rumor so terrible that all other talk stopped: Charles Hardenbergh was dying.

Nothing, of course, could happen in the master's quarters without the slaves learning about it. What news they failed to pick up while going about their work, they picked up in grisly detail from Soan, who had the job of nursing the sick man. The master had been in bed for a month. Recently Soan had returned to the dark cellar, shaking her head. "He don't even open his eyes any more. And his nose pokes up so thin and sharp on the pillow. Looks more like the blade of an ax than it do any man's nose I ever saw."

The slaves in the cellar had only one thought: "What will happen to us if master dies?" They all knew that an old master was better than a new one. That was why, as Charles Hardenbergh lay dying, his slaves prayed that he might live. They prayed for their sakes, not his.

Now more often than ever, Ma-Ma took to sitting down with Belle and Peter, pulling their wiry little bodies as close to her as she could, and Belle, who was about eleven, sometimes would notice Ma-Ma's eyes filling with tears. Never had Belle seen her face look so sad, except perhaps when her mother spoke of the lost children. But Ma-Ma's voice always stayed firm and quiet. At last, one night, she said, "Now, Belle, and you, Pete, I want you both always to remember the things I am going to tell you tonight, even if I have told them to you before. For you'll be told many things after I am gone. . . ."

As her mother's low, throaty voice trailed off for a moment, Belle's heart gave a queer jump. Where was Ma-Ma going? But her mother continued immediately. "I just want to tell you both again—you, Peter, are you listening to me?—I want to tell you always do like your Ma-Ma says today. Promise me again never to lie or steal but always to obey your master. And if your master is bad or mean to you, remember to just ask God to make him good. God'll hear you even though he's far up in the sky. And he'll do it, too, if you remember to ask."

And there in the dark, as she had so often before, Ma-Ma had Peter and Belle kneel and say the Lord's Prayer. But this time she had the children repeat the words over and over in Low Dutch until she was quite sure they knew them by heart.

Later, lying on the damp straw in the cellar, Belle wondered—if God was always so willing to help, why had not Ma-Ma asked him to stop selling her children? But Belle did not find too much time to think about that, because that same night the slaves' worst fears came true. Charles Hardenbergh died. Seven days later a notice was posted in nearby Kingston: "the slaves, horses, and other cattle of Charles Hardenbergh, deceased" would be sold at auction to the highest bidder on the following Tuesday.

Now the War Begun

T W O

ॐ On the auction stand above Belle stood a fat man in a top
hat and frock coat, legs spread out to either side like thick roots
supporting a short, squat trunk. He had his back to the slaves,
while from his mouth poured a torrent of sing-song syllables
aimed at the crowd of well-dressed people in front. As he chanted,
he swayed back and forth, from time to time making a sudden
lunge forward, fat finger pointed like a blunt arrow at a face in
the crowd. Then back he would roll on his heels, swaying in
place.

That endless chant made Belle's grip tighten hard around

Peter's hand. She heard her brother whimper, "Let go!" But she paid no mind. She did not understand the words flowing from the mouth of the fat man on the stand. They came too fast. Yet the words made her pull in her head like a turtle, as if they were huge hailstones chopping their way through summer leaves.

Every so often the wooden gavel in the man's hand would come down on the table in front of him with such a crack! Belle expected to see the board split in two. Then for a moment the words would cease. Through the short field grass would come the shuffle of feet—horses' feet, or cows', or sheep's, or pigs'. Or a slave, standing alongside the auctioneer, would climb down at the front of the platform and disappear behind a man Belle had never seen before. She looked anxiously around for Ma-Ma and Bome-free.

Then Peter's hand was no longer in Belle's. Belle had stood up. The auctioneer was waving her up three wooden steps. Something peculiar had happened to her legs. Were the steps really so steep? She was on the platform. There, in front, were the chatting ladies and gentlemen, the farmers, and the townfolk. There were the laughing white children chasing each other over the grass. Belle never saw them. She saw only blurred streaks of color across a familiar green field.

"Going, going, GONE!"

For the last time, Belle heard the crack of the wooden gavel. She herself was moving across the grass now, listening to the shuffle of her own bare feet, and being shoved along by a strange arm. She looked around wildly for Ma-Ma and Bomefree. They were there by the gate. She heard Bomefree's whisper: "I'll be by to see you, Belle. Don't you worry!" She felt Ma-Ma's arms around her, tight and warm. Then the strange arm shoved her through the gate.

The morning Belle was sold, her mother and father had been freed. The Hardenbergh heirs had known from the first they could not get a penny for old Bomefree. What was left to buy in that worked-out body? But the law forbade a master to free any slave unless he "appeared to be" under fifty years of age and "of sufficient ability to provide for himself." Bomefree hardly answered that description. If they freed Bomefree, the Hardenberghs would have to post bond, but no one wanted to put up the money. Then someone thought of freeing Ma-Ma. Still young and strong, she could care for Bomefree and be his bond. It would satisfy the law.

"Freedom." A word to be whispered in the slave cellar. A thing that a slave could never quite hope to touch, but only dream about, long for. Belle saw tears pour down her parents' faces that morning. The joy was so great, it seemed more like sorrow.

"Belle, we'll be coming to see you. Won't be any master telling us where to be from now on."

It had seemed wonderful. In fact, until she had found herself

During Belle's childhood, advertisements offering slaves for sale frequently appeared in New York State papers.

For Sale,

A LIKELY, HEALTHY, YOUNG
NEGRO WENCH,

BETWEEN fifteen and sixteen Years old : She has been used to the Farming Business. Sold for want of Employ.—Enquire at No. 81, William-street.

New-York, March 30, 1789.

behind that auctioneer's stand, Belle had almost forgotten she and Peter were not to be freed, too.

Now, several hours later, she was stumbling down a dusty road, trailing a flock of sheep. Behind the sheep and the girl strode a hawk-nosed man, barking orders impatiently in a language she could not understand.

Belle's new master, John Neely, was reasonably content that day. He had picked up a flock of healthy sheep and a sturdy looking slave child, all for one hundred dollars. Not a bad bargain.

He had intended to buy only some sheep. But when the auctioneer offered to throw the child in with them—well, John Neely had never owned a slave. Still, owning one could do the Neelys no harm so long as they had to live in Ulster County. Most people of any consequence in the county owned at least one. As strangers —English-speaking Yankees, at that—it was especially important for the Neelys to show that they approved of local customs.

The Neelys came from Massachusetts. Slavery had been abolished there, of course. Owning a black girl would be clear proof now that the Neelys sided with the Dutch on the question of abolition. It would be good for business. That was important because John Neely had a new business, not an easy thing to start among strangers. Only last month he had placed an announcement in the county paper:

NEW STORE AND LANDING: Lately erected about a mile above William Swart's, known by the name of Twaalf-kill, 1-1/2 miles from Kingston Village. John Neely takes this method to acquaint the public that he has for sale at the above store a general assortment of European and West India goods, American and German STEEL, suedes and common IRON, etc., which he is determined to sell at uncommon low prices, either for Cash, Lumber, or any kind of merchantable produce for which he intends to allow the highest market price.

At the bottom of his announcement Neely had been careful to point out:

N.B. The above landing is not only to be preferred to either of the above Kingston landings, on account of it being nearer to the village, but the road to it is so much better and easier as hardly to admit of comparison.

If Kingston folk had any practical sense—and the Dutch were said to have more than their share of that—Neely's announcement was bound to bring customers in. True, he had had very little response as yet. It would take a while to change the habits of country folk. After all, they had been trading for years at the other two landings where they could chat across the counter in Low Dutch. Neely understood Dutch well enough, but unfortunately he spoke hardly a word of it.

On the other hand, every word of the announcement in the *Kingston Argus* had been true. The new landing was closer to the village. The road was better. And his prices were right. The Dutch were slower to get moving than an ox stuck in a bog. But just give them time. They would come around.

He jabbed his stick into the flank of an erring sheep. Too many Yankees were swarming into the county. That was the real trouble! People resented them. All day long you could hear the sound of Yankee axes clearing the hemlock from the slopes. From dawn to dusk the echoes ran up and down the length of the valley.

Neely had come to Ulster County for the same reason other

Yankees had. Men were out of work in New England. Many were losing their farms because they could not pay the high taxes levied to settle war debts. Men looked longingly toward New York, where hundreds of miles of land still lay untouched. Neely, a storekeeper, had watched his customers move away one by one. Finally he himself had felt forced to follow.

Most new arrivals either climbed into the hills behind the Hudson or moved farther west into the state. But a storekeeper needed a town. Neely had chosen to settle in a Dutch community. It was not easy. Yankees were not popular among the Dutch. But perhaps the new slave would help matters a little.

At any rate, he reflected, Mrs. Neely should be pleased. Being a slaveowner would give her a bit more standing in the eyes of local ladies.

The black girl was stumbling again. Neely swung his stick impatiently, striking Belle sharply on the calf. This one, too, spoke only Dutch. That would certainly not be to Mrs. Neely's liking. She understood even less of the language than he did.

He shrugged his shoulders, gripping the stick even more firmly as they turned in at his gate. "Now, now," he thought. "No need to worry, Mrs. Neely. The girl'll pick up English fast enough." If she proved slow, John Neely knew ways to knock the Dutch out of her.

"What on earth have ye got there, John Neely?"

Belle's new mistress had a face as thin and sharp as her husband's. Her black skirt and white blouse were severely neat, her movements abrupt, and her high, complaining voice, with its unfamiliar words, cut into Belle's ears like the whine of a saw on a wet log.

Neely tried a big jovial grin. But he had not used it in such a long time it seemed to pinch the corners of his mouth.

"Bought the sheep, like I set out to do. And bought ye a black girl to boot. They wouldn't sell me the sheep without her. She's a mite young and none too plump. But 'pears strong enough." He gestured with his stick. "There ye are, Mrs. Neely. Got yourself a slave."

He took a breath. "Only one trouble, she's another of these Dutch'uns. Don't 'pear to know a word of English."

Mrs. Neely looked at Belle distrustfully. She saw nothing that she liked in the slender, bony thing standing before her, with frightened, downcast eyes, rubbing one dusty bare foot against the other.

The Yankee woman snorted. "What's the difference whether I like it or not, John Neely. Ye've gone and done it, ain't ye? Just get her on in here. We'll soon enough find out what she's good for."

Many years later, Sojourner Truth said of that day, "Now the war begun."

Mrs. Neely was all efficiency. A brisk, impatient woman, she darted around her kitchen, delivering sharp orders in her whiny voice and strange language.

Belle had never been addressed except in Low Dutch, for although most Ulster County Dutch knew English they seldom used it at home and never to a slave. Now Belle was expected not only to understand the new language, but to leap like a hare to obey her mistress's every command.

"Belle, the frying pan," she would snap over her shoulder. Nothing stirred behind her. Mrs. Neely would turn around. The frightened, confused look on Belle's face seemed only to infuriate her mistress.

"The frying pan!" she would scream, in a voice loud enough to jar the dishes from the shelves. Mrs. Neely clearly believed the only way to reach a child's mind was to blast her way in.

Could Mrs. Neely be asking for the pothooks? Belle would run to fetch them. Oh, what a slapping! And evenings, when John Neely came home, what an earful of angry complaints he would get. Sometimes, to prove his sympathy for his wife as much as anything, Neely would take Belle outside and add another beating to whatever cuffs she had collected during the day.

Neely began to enjoy this method of soothing his wife. Business at the new landing was not picking up as he had hoped. It was hard enough for an honest American to have to listen to Dutch all day. Did he have to put up with it even in his own home? Oh, he would teach this one the language of the nation, sure enough.

At least Belle had plenty to eat. As in all small northern homes with only one or two slaves, the slave ate at the table with his owners and shared their fare. Mrs. Neely set a good table and did not stint any who sat with her.

But soon winter came—a bitter winter that year. Snow hardened in white ridges along the bare branches of oak and beech and walnut, and sank deep into the sagging arms of hemlock and white pine. All winter long Belle ached with cold. She had only one dress, the same she had worn all summer—a shabby square-cut garment made from a single width of tow cloth. (This was rough material woven from broken, leftover strands of flax and so commonly used for slave's clothing that it was called "slave cloth.") This dress, a pair of broken shoes, and a castoff shawl of Mrs. Neely's were Belle's winter clothing.

It was true that she worked mostly in the house. But there was wood to be carried in, and there were sheep and cows to look after. And even the house was cold, except where the great open fireplaces shed a half-circle of warmth.

But the little girl remembered that winter for another reason: it was the year she got the worst beating of her life. Belle never knew just what she had done wrong. Possibly the Neelys had simply decided it was time to "beat the Dutch" out of her.

Belle was told to go to the barn. There she found her master with a bundle of slender wooden rods in one hand. They had been turned in the embers, one by one, until they were perfectly smooth and hard. Then Neely had tied them tightly together with cord. His face in the dim barn light looked as hard and tight as the rods. He ordered Belle to bare her back. Then he tied her hands together so she could not ward off the blows. And then he whipped her.

He was a wiry man. And he was angry at so many things. Angry at the Dutch farmers. Angry at the way his business was going. Angry that he had had to leave his home in New England and come among strangers. Angry at the black child who refused to speak English. Angry that his wife blamed him for everything.

After the rods had finished rising and falling, rising and falling, Belle lay a long time on the rough wooden floor of the barn. As she lay there she seemed to see her mother's face drawing near, with its great sorrowful eyes. She reached toward it, but the face retreated again. To reappear. And retreat. And reappear.

Then the voice of Mrs. Neely rasped through her dream. "Belle, git back in here and git to work."

Footprints in the Snow

THREE

෩ Later that day, as soon as she could escape Mrs. Neely, Belle ran out the kitchen door, across two fields, and behind a screen of white birches. She had been there many times before. She turned her face trustingly toward the sky as to an old friend. Her voice came so loud, it almost shook the snow from the branches.

"God, was it right for him to do that? Was it right?" The field was quiet while she waited for an answer, her broad-cheeked, firm little face pointed pleadingly at the sky.

Ma-Ma had described God to Belle as a Mighty Being who lived in the sky. Belle talked to him now almost every day. For one thing there was no one else to whom she could speak in Low Dutch. And had not Ma-Ma promised, "God will always hear you and help you, Belle, when you ask him."

She had been lucky to find this spot away from the house, where she could be alone and shout to God without fear of being overheard. Time after time she had cried up to him, "Please make my master and my mistress good." But, as she admitted years later, "It didn't seem to do no good."

Perhaps making people as bad as the Neelys "good" was too big a job, even for God. So after some months Belle decided it might be more sensible to ask smaller favors. However, as she said later, "When I was to get beaten, I never knew it long enough before-hand to pray. And yet I always believed if I only had had time to ask God for help, I could have escaped the beating."

At any rate, she had had no time to ask help that cold morning that John Neely called her out to the barn. And now, after asking, "Was it right for him to do that?" she stood even longer than usual waiting for her answer—a slender, dark child, alone against the snow. Her back burned and her loneliness seemed almost to burst her heart. Sometimes she sang her shouts to God. Today she could not sing. Yet, despite her pain, there was no answer from the sky.

What could Belle do? It was hard not having anyone to talk to. Even Bomefree had failed her. He had promised to come to see her, but she had been waiting for months and her father had not come . . . perhaps that was what she could do. She could ask God to make her father come. Bomefree was free now, Belle reminded herself fiercely. He *had* to come. He had to find some way to help his little girl. Her voice rose and fell in the way she had so often heard Ma-Ma's voice rise and fall, as Belle repeated over and over her prayer to God.

A few days later she was putting wood on the fire, when she

heard a knock outside. It was her father, standing in the snow. Belle wasn't surprised for she believed quite simply that God had answered her prayers. She clamped her arms around Bomefree's twisted form as if nothing could ever separate them again. Tears stung her eyes at the smell of the damp old cellar clinging to his shabby coat. How was Ma-Ma? Had he seen Peter?

Ma-Ma was well. Peter? "I don't expect ever to see my boy again, Belle. My legs are too stiff now to travel so far." "The only reason I could come today," he added, "was because the man living in Master Charles's house offered me a ride. I can't stay long. Right now he's down at the landing. I'm to meet him at the crossing on his way back."

Bomefree's gentle, warm eyes searched his daughter's unhappy face. "White folks treatin' you all right, Belle?" His stiff fingers stroked her cheek.

She wanted to answer, but her throat was too tight to let the words through. "Well," Bomefree said at last. "Looks like they're feeding you pretty good anyhow." He seemed uneasy.

"Oh, yes," mumbled Belle. "Plenty to eat." She did not dare start pouring out her troubles to him. Mrs. Neely kept walking in and out of the room, her sharp nose twitching like an alerted rabbit's. The woman would not leave the pair alone for a minute.

Soon Bomefree rose to go. Belle's hands clutched at his sleeve as she followed him to the gate. There she could no longer hold back her tears. In the shadow of the hedge, beyond the darting eyes and gaping ears of her mistress, she pulled down her dress to show him her scarred back. "Oh, Daddy, can't you do something to get me a new master?"

She had never seen such an angry look on Bomefree's face. For a moment it seemed the face of a much younger man. His fingers traced the fresh welts running along his daughter's shoulders, and the angry look grew hard. "I'll see what I can do, Belle," he promised. He pulled her rough dress gently back into place. "Just wait, child. I'll see what I can do."

The old man moved jerkily up the dirt road toward the crossing. His head was down, but he turned once to wave encouragingly at the small figure watching from the gate. At that distance he could not see that she had planted both her feet in the two huge footprints he had left in the snow where they had last stood talking together.

Long after he disappeared she remained like that, staring at his tracks that led up the road from Mrs. Neely's house.

The next morning Belle returned to the spot where she had parted from her father. Again she placed her feet carefully inside the long wide prints carved by that tall man's feet. Very carefully she walked in his tracks up the road, clear up to the place he had turned for the last time to wave good-bye. There Belle raised her voice. "God, please help my father get me a good master and mistress. God, you've got to help him," she bellowed.

She did this every day, until Bomefree's footprints had vanished in the melting snow. Only a few white patches now remained in the fields, the wet brown earth showing between them. Buds bulged like stubby caterpillars on the knobby gray branches of trees.

A man walked up to Mrs. Neely's door. Belle was alone. "Would you like to come live with me?" he asked in Dutch. Her startled eyes fastened on the open, good-natured face and the rough clothing. She thought of Mrs. Neely's tight face, poking around corners, its nose twitching with distrust. She thought of John Neely's cold eyes as he held the smooth rods in his hand and of his arm rising and falling above her. She knew her prayer had been answered.

"Yes," she said.

Growing Wild

FOUR

ई☙ In less time than it would have taken her to break an egg into Mrs. Neely's frying pan, Belle was ready to go. She had nothing to pack. Not even the tow-cloth garment she wore belonged to her. The man had heard of Belle from Bomefree; he bought her and the dress from John Neely for one hundred and five dollars.

"Come along with me, then," he ordered cheerfully, and mounting a sturdy, dappled mare he trotted off up the road toward the ferry.

Belle scampered along, far enough behind to keep free of the horse's hooves but not so far she did not find she had to duck now and then to avoid the clumps of wet earth the animal sent sailing past her ear. Only once did she bother to glance back. As she rounded the first bend, she turned for a last, long look.

For a moment her face was sullen. Mrs. Neely knew that look. "Belle's look," she would sniff in exasperation. Under the lash of Mrs. Neely's tongue or the slap of Mrs. Neely's hand, Belle's mouth would pout and her head droop.

But now when Belle raised her head to hurry along after the stranger's horse, her face was eager. "Thank you, God," she murmured.

It was a short, easy trot for the mare to the home of Belle's new master, and not much more difficult for the sturdy young girl. After a mile they were at the ferry, where they crossed Rondout Creek. Then they went another half a mile up the road. Every step was a step farther from the old life, a step nearer the new. Of one thing Belle could be sure: this time the new master had to be better than the old.

Martin Schryver was a fisherman, a tavernkeeper, and, last of all, a farmer. A jovial, outgoing man, he especially enjoyed keeping tavern. Belle could usually find him leaning over the long counter of the bar, surrounded by smells of hard cider, beer-soaked wooden kegs, Ulster County grain whiskey, and West Indian rum. Belle's new master would cheerfully have traded gossip and news twenty-four hours a day with the farmers, sailors, and hired hands who wandered into the tavern. Most of these, like Schryver himself, were simple folk, rough-mannered but with warm enough hearts.

As for Schryver's farming, that took little of his time. He had a large farm, but for the most part it was not even cleared. A patch here was planted in corn. Over there lay a field of wheat. A few vegetables and some fruit trees straggled behind the house. Several hogs, a scattering of chickens, three cows, and some sheep, all roaming wherever they wished—that was about the sum of Martin Schryver's farming.

As for the fishing, he left that to his sons. It was enough to keep them out of trouble the year around.

Later Belle recalled her year with the Schryvers as a contented one. They treated the young slave as kindly as they would have any young farm animal, and they were kindly people. In fact Belle began to wonder if freedom might not be something like belonging to the Schryvers.

Her wiry body thrived on the wild outdoor life she led. "Help the boys bring up the fish, Belle," Schryver would yell out. And she would scurry down to the creek to pull squirming silver bodies out of the bottom of the boat. When the oak leaves got to be about "as big as a squirrel's foot," it was time to be in the fields, thrusting grains of hard yellow corn into cool black soil, remembering to plant pumpkin seeds between every hill of corn. When the soil began to feel warm under her bare feet, the cry was, "Corn needs hoeing." And she would work at that for long hours in the hot summer sun. Or she would hear, "Beer's almost gone, Belle. Pick some hops." Alone in the silent, dark woods, Belle would seek out the wild hops that sprang up in tangled underbrush. And almost any moment of the year she could expect the bellow to burst from Mrs. Schryver's powerful lungs, "Sweetenin' jug's empty." Then off would trot "Schryver's Belle," lugging the empty crock to the Strand where the storekeeper would fill it to the brim with dark, heavy molasses.

And always she was singing, singing the songs that Ma-Ma had sung in those words that no one understood. Or sometimes making up her own words as she struggled with the slippery fish or peered through the undergrowth for the hops. But now not so many of her songs were meant for God. She did not need her Mighty Being so much here. In fact, instead of prayers she was learning a few curse words; the Schryvers were pretty good at that.

She was thirteen and full of energy. The work seemed like nothing. Moreover, as she remembered later, there was always plenty of time at the Schryver's to just browse around. In summer that meant sitting on the pier down at the Strand, watching the Hudson River sloops with their great sails and towering masts turn up Rondout Creek. Each boat's broad bow bulged like the head of some huge fish. As the sailors unloaded she would see that head rise higher and higher out of the water. And what treasures came up from the great fish's belly. Warm flannel cloth, and coffee, and tea. Salt, sugar, and West Indian rum. Iron nails. Furniture and kitchen tools.

Other days, as she watched, the sailors would be loading the hold again for the return trip to New York. Flour and whiskey it was now, and dressed skins, potatoes, cabbages, and sun-dried fruits. And the great head would sink slowly back into the creek.

In winter there were no sloops to watch. The river lay frozen and quiet while heavily loaded sleighs and stagecoaches on silver runners raced up and down the ice. Bells jingled from horses' bridles. Passengers huddled, red-nosed, buried under buffalo hides and thick bearskins. Sometimes Belle would tie smooth beef bones to her feet and skate, or coast downhill on the curved wooden staves of a broken barrel.

And she continued to grow. One morning as the tall young girl loped through the vegetable patch, Mrs. Schryver happened to glance up at her. "Lawd, Martin," she exclaimed to her husband. "That black gal's shootin' up like a new sprout on a willow. Just look at all that skin shinin' between her dress and her knee. It ain't decent."

As Belle told it many years later, "A slave got a strip of slave's cloth, just so long, and had to wear it width-wise. Them that was short got along pretty well, but as for me . . ." and she would look wryly down her long body. Belle solved the problem quite simply by sewing the cloth up between the legs, rather like bloomers today. In those days it was a strange dress.

At thirteen she was already six feet tall and straight as a sapling, towering over most of the men who entered the tavern. But folks turned to notice for more reasons than that. Her long, loping stride reminded many of a powerful colt. Her face was broad and strong with its generous mouth and high-bridged nose. Recently she had started to wear a madras bandanna to hold the tangled hair back out of her eyes; on a young Negro girl, a bandanna was a sign of womanhood.

But Martin Schryver noticed few of these changes. He was far too busy in the tavern, exchanging friendly gossip with customers. In fact, Mrs. Schryver had been complaining lately that her Martin gave away as many drinks as he sold. But she was as good-natured as he; her complaints usually ended in a wry, helpless shrug. While there were fish in the river and seed ready to fall and take root on the land, she supposed the Schryvers would never starve. And yet. . . .

One afternoon, a tall gentleman trotted his horse off the ferry that crossed the creek below, dismounted at the tavern, asked for a drink—and casually offered three hundred dollars for Belle. Mrs. Schryver's shoulders froze in the middle of a shrug. Her eyes seemed to hook Martin by the collar as they motioned him firmly to her end of the bar.

"Well, now," he murmured, scratching his head with the long nail he kept on his index finger, "I don't rightly know about sellin' her. She's a good wench and does as she's told. We'd only have to look for another."

"But three hundred dollars, Martin Schryver. Three hundred dollars!" Mrs. Schryver argued. "Do you realize that's three times what you paid for her? You're not goin' to turn that kind of money down, are you, you crazy tavern keeper?"

"Well," Martin squirmed uneasily. "I just don't know. Next gal might not be as good. This one's handy and quick. She don't get in the way of customers. And she sings real pretty. Don't lie or steal." He seemed to be working himself up to something. His wife waited. Suddenly, Martin folded his arms. "Nope. I'm not sellin' her."

Mrs. Schryver pretended she hadn't heard the last sentence. "What you say's all true, Martin Schryver. All true. But, still and all, you just can't go turnin' down money like that when we need it so bad." Her voice underlined every word as firmly as if the voice itself had been the thick stick of charcoal with which she normally figured up a bill. She was leaning forward on her hands across the bar, her arms spread wide on the counter. Her eyes never left her husband's face.

Martin sighed.

And so, once more, Belle found herself trotting barefoot up a road behind a new master.

Mighty Being

F I V E

෧෨ The man and the girl were passing through a stretch of forest that afternoon, when the new master reined in his horse. As he looked back at her, his face and shoulders were framed against the sky.

"Are you tired, gal?"

Belle shook her head. She was not tired. But her legs trembled like swamp reeds in a storm. The sun was already low behind the trees. Shadows shifted in the woods, and the tall man against the sky was a stranger.

Belle stole a sidelong glance at the muscular arm reining in the

horse. She imagined it raised up in rage, like the arm of John
Neely. She thought of Mrs. Neely and the straining tendons in her
neck. And she tried to imagine what the mistress might be like
who waited now at the end of this road.

She struggled to keep the fear off her face. White folk never
cared to see anything but cheerful looks on a slave. Why only the
other day, a neighbor of Schryver's had whipped his slave to
death. A mean master, everyone said. But folks said, too, that a
slave should know better than to wear a sad look for such a long
time after his wife was sold away. Should have known his master
wouldn't like it.

The white man's horse had trotted ahead again. Belle stole
another timid glance. This man did not appear to be so mean. But
until she had seen him angry, she would not really know him. She
found herself softly repeating Ma-Ma's instructions, "Work hard
to please your master. Don't lie. Don't steal." She rolled the words

*As she went from new master to new master, the child Belle traveled many
miles over rutted Ulster roads like this one.*

COURTESY NEW YORK HISTORICAL SOCIETY

over and over her tongue like a charm. But the fear inside her could not be so easily charmed away.

The horse ahead whinnied and his hooves scrambled faster over the dirt. He had turned up a side road. Belle could see the Hudson, and crowning the heights above the river was a snug stone house with a steep roof. Next to the house was a barn just like Charles Hardenbergh's—a typical Dutch barn, as big as a church.

The new master waved his arm at the fields and woods around. "This is my land," he said. Then he stopped trying to hold his impatient horse down to a walk. The horse flew up the road, and the man leaped to the ground in front of the house. A slender woman came out to greet him, followed by a girl with long blond hair falling down her back who seemed a little younger than Belle. Belle's feet dragged in the dirt of the road as she moved slowly toward the group standing outside the house. She was measuring all three with her eyes.

That evening John J. Dumont of New Paltz took out his account book. Puffing on his pipe, he carefully noted that he had purchased from Martin Schryver, tavern keeper, that day in 1810, a slave girl known as Isabelle who appeared to be about thirteen years old, although unusually tall for her age.

By New York standards John Dumont was a large slaveholder. He owned ten slaves. Like many others of his kind, he housed them—men, women, and children—all together in a single large room located directly behind the regular kitchen and called the slave kitchen.

Some of Dumont's slaves worked in the fields, others worked around the house or tended the farm animals. Belle was to work in the kitchen and help Mrs. Dumont. If she had time she would be used elsewhere as well.

From the start John Dumont was delighted with his new purchase. Mrs. Dumont was not. In fact, Mrs. Dumont seemed particularly to resent John Dumont's delight. Belle had been there only a few weeks when she overheard her master exclaim to a friend: "You should see that gal work. She'll do the work of half a dozen other slaves—and do it better too."

Belle noticed her mistress stiffen with displeasure. "None of Belle's work is ever more than half done," she said icily.

Mrs. Dumont had a manner as calm as the water of Rondout Creek on a still November day. She never raised her voice. But her words were as cold as the icy water of that creek.

Belle also had to deal with Kate, a white orphan a few years older than Belle. Kate was a bond servant from the county poorhouse. A bond servant was only a notch above a slave. Kate received no pay, only food and clothing. The county saved money by putting her out to work for Mrs. Dumont. But when Kate had worked out her time, she would be free, like any other white American—free to go where she wanted.

Meanwhile, the difference between Kate and Belle was not so very wide. But Kate and Mrs. Dumont aimed to have it look as wide as possible. Whatever Kate did to emphasize her superiority seemed to delight Mrs. Dumont. Mrs. Dumont never seemed to be looking when Kate would trip Belle with her broom or "accidentally" knock the sugar bowl from the young slave's hand. "Don't be so clumsy, Belle," Mrs. Dumont would say.

"It's like having two mistresses," Belle fretted. "And both mean."

Fortunately, Belle very soon found a friend. Dumont's daughter Gertrude took more after her father than she did after her mother. A quiet, firm-minded child, she had no one to play with around the house and liked to chat with Belle in the kitchen or help her cut up vegetables for the stew. But if Kate was there,

Gertrude wouldn't come in. "She's always trying to tell me what to do," she told Belle resentfully.

It was Belle's job also to clean Gertrude's room. When Mrs. Dumont was around, this had to be done fast; Mrs. Dumont, whose own family had not used slaves, didn't like a slave loitering in her daughter's room. But sometimes Mrs. Dumont was away and then Belle could take time to examine the expensively dressed dolls on Gertrude's bed or look at the school books with their mysterious black and white pages.

Belle's difficulties with Mrs. Dumont and Kate came to a peak before very long. The family was fond of boiled potatoes for breakfast. One morning Belle had set a bowlful on the dining-room table as usual and had returned to the kitchen, when she heard her mistress's voice rise sharply in the next room.

"Now, Mr. Dumont, there's a perfect sample of your Belle's work." Through the door, Belle could see Mrs. Dumont's finger pointing triumphantly at the table.

"Belle," her master sounded surprised. "Why do the potatoes look so dirty?"

Belle's puzzled eyes scrutinized the potatoes. How had they come to be so gray? She looked helplessly at Dumont. "I made the potatoes my usual way, master."

Dumont looked impatient. "We can't have things like this happening," he complained. "Please be more careful in the future."

His scolding frightened Belle, but it had no effect on the potatoes. Three mornings in a row they turned up at breakfast as dirty-looking as if Belle had rolled them, in deliberate defiance, one by one, down the center of the kitchen floor. Every morning John Dumont's warnings grew angrier and Mrs. Dumont's face more smug.

After Belle's third scolding from Dumont, Gertrude came into the kitchen to find the tall young slave standing against the wall, hands clenched, black eyes staring, as if undecided in what direction to flee. Gertrude placed a hand on one of Belle's clenched fists. "Belle, I can't stand to hear them talk to you that way. I know it can't be your fault. Maybe together we could find out what's happening."

Belle agreed to wake Gertrude next morning, and before dawn the two sat down side by side to wash and peel the breakfast potatoes. When the pot had been put on to boil, Belle left the kitchen as she did each day to go to the barn and milk the cow.

She had just closed the door softly behind her, in order not to wake those sleeping upstairs, when Kate walked in.

"Gert, what are you doing up so early?" Kate asked. She was obviously annoyed but her angry look changed as quickly to a smile. "Well, as long as you're here, Gert, be a love. Run down to the cellar and fetch me a jar of pickles."

Gert shook her head, stubbornly keeping her eye on Kate. When Kate saw there was to be no cooperation, she picked up the hearth broom. "Get out of my way then," she snapped. "I have my work to do." And she began energetically sweeping the ashes from the hearth. As if by accident, a broomful of dirt sailed into the potatoes.

Gert shot up from her stool. "I saw you," she screamed.

"You saw me what?" asked Kate.

But Gert was gone. Her long braid flying behind her, she was tearing through the house to find her father.

Despite the happy ending, Belle's close call with Dumont's displeasure only increased her anxiety to please him. Supposing she should finally lose his protection? What would happen, with Mrs. Dumont so full of hate for her? Belle vowed to redouble her efforts to make sure she could never again forfeit Dumont's favor. What a relief it was, soon after, to again hear him boasting: "That wench is better to me than a man. She'll do a good family's wash in the night, and by morning she'll be ready to go into the fields where she'll do as much raking and binding as my best field hand."

Sometimes, intoxicated by such praise from her master, Belle would refuse her complaining body its rest, forcing herself to work on through the night. Only when she could work no more, would she lean for a moment to rest against the wall. And often, leaning there, she would fall asleep and never know it until her head hit the floor.

Such peculiar behavior soon got Belle into trouble with Dumont's other slaves. One day Dumont's driver, an old slave known as Cato who also acted as a preacher, took Belle aside.

"What's the matter with you, gal? Can't you see you only hurtin' the rest of us when you work yourself to death like you doin'? Next thing we know, master'll be expectin' us all to work like that. Where'll we find time to take care of our own children then? When us old people gonna rest? Workin' hard ain't gonna free *any* of us. Just kill us sooner, that's all. You're smart, gal. You should know better than that."

But Belle would not listen. The several years she had spent away from other slaves had weakened her ties to her own people. She was proud to be her master's favorite slave. His pride in her was more important than anything else.

"White man's pet!" She grew used to hearing the phrase hissed after her as she passed. It frightened her to feel their disapproval, but it was better than risking her master's. When the slaves jeered at her, she would wrap her long arms tightly around herself and rock quietly back and forth, comforting herself with the notion that Ma-Ma at least, if she knew, would approve of her obedience and hard work.

The more the slaves criticized her, the more stubborn Belle grew. At last she worked herself into such a state of righteousness, she even convinced herself that John Dumont was the Mighty

Being whom Ma-Ma had said lived high in the sky. Had not Ma-Ma Betts promised that the Mighty Being would protect her against a bad mistress?

This thought made Belle feel even more superior to the other slaves. She was her master's favorite and her master was the Lord. She now went about her tasks feeling quite certain that she had been especially chosen from among all the slaves of Ulster County to do the Lord's work. She no longer even noticed what the other slaves said about her. What did they know? Ignorant black folk!

And yet, what slave did not dream about freedom? At night even Belle dreamed those forbidden dreams, remembering her family and forgetting, while she slept, all the reasons she gave herself in the day for being better off with Dumont. But in the day, she put the dream away again, like a thought that could only scald her and deprive her of her master's protection.

But the dream would not die. She was still very young, and in her loneliness, Belle began longing to see her mother. She had not seen her since the day she was eleven years old, when they had been separated at Hardenbergh's auction. As slaves figured those things, that was three masters ago—a long time.

The more Belle thought about her mother, the more homesick she became, until she found herself constantly planning how she could get back to Hurley once more. She thought Dumont would permit it, but there was a great deal of work to do. She waited for the right moment to ask him.

Then one day John Dumont ordered old Cato to drive Belle over to Hurley in the farm wagon. She was to see her mother again, but not as she had wished.

"Your ma's dead, Belle," said the old preacher. "Master says I should take you to see her before she's buried, if you want to go."

As old Cato flicked the reins on the bay horse's neck, the farm wagon rolled swiftly over the dirt roads. It rocked from side to side over the stretch Belle had walked behind John Dumont, just three years earlier, and jiggled and jounced over the short piece she had trotted behind Martin Schryver and over the rutted miles she and the sheep had plodded, urged on by the stick in John Neely's hand. And all the way, as she and Cato retraced each road she had traveled since the day of Charles Hardenbergh's auction, Belle could see Ma-Ma's happy, hopeful face on that last morning they had spent together.

Soon Belle was back in Hurley, sitting again on the steps of the damp cellar where she had spent so many nights of her childhood. But now Belle was sixteen years old, a grown woman, her master's favorite slave, trying in vain to comfort an old man, her father, who was "free."

Bomefree's back seemed even more bent, his fingers more twisted than she had remembered. Under the dirt his matted hair and beard were as white as the linen Belle washed and bleached in the sun for Mrs. Dumont. Tears streaked the dust on his dark cheeks.

"I stumbled against something on the cellar floor, Belle. I felt it with my hands. It was your ma. Her body was cold." The old man began to weep uncontrollably.

Years later, Sojourner Truth described parting from her father that day. "Oh, how he cried! Aloud, like a child. Poor old man. I remember his cry as if it were but yesterday."

That day the cry seemed to trail her all the way back to Dumont's. One moment, as the wagon jounced along, the sound came rushing at her from a wood. The next moment it rose from a brook bubbling close to the road. Then, lonely and forlorn, it rolled, endlessly long, across a great stretch of silent meadow.

Growing Pains

SIX

꿍 One day, about that time, Belle was stopped on the road by a tall man with a gentle face who placed his hand quietly on her arm, saying, "It is not right thee should be a slave. It is not according to God's will. Soon there will be a law to free thee."

She bounded away like a frightened deer to tell Dumont. She was convinced her master could read the thoughts of all his slaves and knew whatever happened to them. She had better tell him herself.

This obsession with her master's good will continued to isolate Belle from her fellow slaves and left her with no one to whom she could confide her daily complaints against Mrs. Dumont and

Kate. When she tried to pour her troubles out to one young woman, she was told, "I ain't listenin' to you, and I ain't tellin' you nothin' neither. White man's pet!"

"White man's pet. White man's pet." She heard that all the time now.

The slaves had reason to be distrustful. There were always spies among them, currying favor with the master by reporting on the other slaves. But Belle was no spy. She curried favor only by telling on herself and by her hard work. The older slaves were wise enough to see that. But the younger ones hadn't enough experience to know. She was a strange one, not easily understood.

Sometimes her loneliness seemed unbearable. One day, in trying to find some way to ease it, she recalled a story she had heard of a soldier who had been left wounded on the field of battle. Alone and hungry, his mouth parched with thirst, he had knelt and prayed so desperately for help that his knees had packed the soft ground under him as hard as a ledge of rock. Then—as if from nowhere—rescuers had appeared. Perhaps now, she thought, if she did as that soldier had done, help would reach her too.

She looked around Dumont's property until she found a small island in the middle of a stream. The island was far enough from the house to be out of earshot, but close enough for her to reach it quickly. Sheep had worn winding paths through its willow shrubbery and water bubbled down the slope, muffling the sound of her voice. She thought it would make a good praying ground.

She used every spare moment to weave the willow branches into a wall thick enough and high enough to hide her body, so that she could tell God all the things she could not tell her master to his face. She believed that in speaking to God, she was speaking to her master, since he was the Mighty Being. But on the island, Belle could speak much more frankly than in Dumont's physical presence.

Yet sometimes, as in her days with Mrs. Neely, her prayers did not seem quickly enough answered. After an especially trying day, she frequently would get quite impatient. "God, why can't you give me a little more help and make it easier for me to be good? If I was you and you was me and you wanted any help, I'd help you. Why can't you help me?"

And she would make God promises. "Yesterday, God, I was so mad at Kate, I just had to take it out on somethin'. I beat the poor cat with a broom. I'm sorry, God, truly sorry. But if you'll just keep Kate and missus away from me, and tell 'em to leave me alone, I'll be absolutely perfect. You'll see I'll do everything exactly right, just the way you want me to. I wouldn't have no more reason not to be good."

Day after day, from deep in her willow grove, Belle fired such promises toward heaven, and day after day, she struggled to keep them, berating herself when night came, feeling that somewhere, in some small way, she had failed again to keep her word.

But her praying ground really eased her loneliness very little. The other slaves still did not trust or like her. She was a young woman alone, in both the white and the black worlds.

Fortunately, even for such a strange one like Belle, life could not be all work and prayer. Every year the changing seasons brought Pinxster to "free" every slave, no matter how dutiful, at least for a little while. Pinxster was the Dutch word for Pentecost. It came fifty days after Easter, and traditionally was a time of joy, hailing the coming of spring. The descendants of the Dutch colonists celebrated Pinxster for an entire week, visiting their neighbors in flower-bedecked wagons, joining in games and festivities. But with time the holiday had come to belong particularly to the slaves. For seven days slaves were given no work to do, and if any slave did work, the master paid for the work as if the slave had been a free man.

Long before dawn on Pinxster Monday slaves could be seen threading their way along the dirt roads that led toward the center of the celebration. Barefooted, wearing slave cloth or some faded, ill-fitting hand-me-down, Belle and the other Dumont slaves headed for the great oak down the way, where the leader of Pinxster waited. Almost seven feet tall, dark, straight, and powerful, Prince Gerald towered above the crowd. Belle had heard it said that his father was a British officer and his mother the daughter of an African king. Although many had tried, no one in the county could outwrestle or outdance that lithe giant. He stood under the great oak, a castoff revolutionary jacket hanging above his naked legs. Colored ribbons dangled from the jacket's brass buttons and a little black hat with a pompon crowned the proud, fine-boned head. His throne was a hollow log, each end covered with tautly drawn skins. As he straddled the log, the tall slave's supple hands kept up a steady drumming. The others accompanied him on eel pots covered with skins. "Hi-a-bomba, bomba," they chanted, as hands clapped and feet stamped and dancers moved in a double-shuffle, or heel-and-toe, or breakdown.

At Pinxster time, the god of the slave owner seemed very far away, even to Belle. Congo gods came to summon the dancers. Congo dancers sent feet kicking up the dust from the road until the lowest leaves turned gray with it. Congo songs burst from throats whose owners did not know what words they sang—any more than Ma-Ma Betts had understood the songs she had sung so long ago. Congo drums beat on and on, all day and all night.

For seven days white people came and watched. Small children stood for hours, open mouthed, only to be carted off at last to their beds. And the dancers whirled on and on. They stopped only to eat the great hunks of fresh summer sausage or ginger bread they had been permitted to make for the occasion, or to tip heavy crocks of last October's cider to their dry lips, or to sleep for a brief hour in the grass. Then up they would rise, and back to the dance.

Pinxster belonged to the slaves. For an entire week, every last one of them could forget to say "Yes, master" or "No, missus." For an entire week, they could forget everything but their own strength and the life pounding in their bodies. They could dance, all of them, as if white men had never come to sell black men into slavery. For one solid week in June there was freedom for everyone, whether black or white. But the black, at that time, seemed more free than the white could ever be.

By the seventh day fewer and fewer were left to whirl and drum on the trampled grass under the great oak. Dancers slept peacefully in the bushes, while aching bare feet carried other dancers back to work over the dirt roads. Wagons creaked along country lanes. For one more year, Pinxster was past.

It was during such a week, one year, that Belle met Robert.

A Man's Life

SEVEN

ॐ Unlike most of the slaves she knew, he was even taller than her own six feet. She had noticed that immediately, as soon as he smiled down at her, his broad-cheeked face shining with the exertion of the dance.

"I'm Bob, from Catlin's place," he had said.

"I'm Belle, from Dumont's." She knew she had made a friend.

That summer, for the first time, Belle could tell her secrets and complain about Mrs. Dumont and Kate to someone who would listen and answer. No season had ever seemed so perfect. The fields were carpeted with wild flowers, while a million slender leaves concealed the willow boughs she had woven into a wall around her praying ground. It was there that she went to meet Bob, because they had to meet in secret. Bob's master had been furious when he learned the reason for his slave's regular visits to Dumont's place.

"Master says he'll kill me if he catches me comin' up here again, Belle," Bob told her bitterly. "He's picked out a gal for me on his own place. He doesn't want your master gettin' my children. Belle, I have to take care. He'd kill me just like he says. He's mean enough to do it."

When she was with Bob, Belle would try not to think about the danger. But she could not always be with him. There was, for instance, the day she fell sick. Her head was pounding and her stomach hurting her so she could hardly bear to rise to her feet. She had sent one of the field hands to tell Bob she could not meet him that day and was lying miserably on her straw pallet, when she heard her master's step in the yard outside the slave kitchen.

"Belle, have you seen Bob?"

She was startled. "No, Master. Bob have no reason to come here."

Dumont frowned. His fingers drummed irritably on the door jamb. "Well, if he should turn up, just tell him to watch his step. The Catlins are looking for him."

He turned to go, then stopped abruptly. Bob stood in the yard, and directly across from Bob stood the Catlins, father and son. Belle heard a scream and knew by the burn in her throat that it was her scream. Even across the yard, she could see her friend's black eyes dilate as he struggled to control his terror.

She heard the rumbling animal shout that came from Catlin. "Knock the black rascal down!" She saw the man and his son both grip their canes by the small end, and she shrank back, trembling, onto her pallet, as the heavy oak ends of those canes rose again and again into the air. She heard Dumont's command: "Stop! I'll have no slave beaten to death on my place."

She saw the younger Catlin snatch a rope from his belt and begin twisting the stunned youth's arms behind his back. Again she heard Dumont's command: "I will not permit any brute to be tied up that way."

The last glimpse she was ever to have of her friend was of a long, half-conscious young body in torn trousers, being dragged across her master's yard.

Some months later she heard that Bob had recovered enough to return to work. During the winter, someone had seen him splitting rails for zig-zag fences. No one knew better than her Bob how to make a fence "horse high and hog tight." Those who had seen him said he had settled down with the young woman his master had chosen for him. Then Belle heard he had died. It was his spirit, people said. The man just never did appear to be the same after that beating; the heart seemed to have gone clean out of him.

Not long after, Belle, too, was forced to settle down. One day Dumont summoned a Negro preacher called King, a slave from a neighboring property, and Belle stood up in front of that preacher, with Thomas, another of her master's slaves, and was married. It was her master's wish.

Belle's new husband was much older than Belle, a short, wizened man with a tired stoop. She was used to his presence; she had seen him for so many years moving slowly around the yard, mending harness, doing odd jobs, or wheezing in his sleep at night in the slave kitchen where they all slept. Tom already had had two wives sold away from him. His eye had little spark, and his spirit sagged from the years of slavery.

But the old man had not always been like that. He was the only slave on Dumont's place who could speak of having run away. That had happened years back when Dumont sold Tom's second wife. Tom had pursued her on foot all the way to New York City. He had tramped the rutted dirt roads and wet swamps, sleeping in the woods at night, dodging behind trees to avoid the wagons that rolled past and the stage coaches with their white passengers jouncing around inside.

On reaching the city, Tom had hidden out for a month in those dark alleys that sheltered so many runaways. But he never had found his wife. Instead, the slave hunters had found Tom and returned him to Dumont. The scars on his back were what remained of his master's greeting to him that day.

About a year after her marriage to Tom, Belle gave birth to her first child, Diana. And not more than a few months after that, the legislature in Albany passed the law that people had been expecting for many years, a law to free all of the state's remaining slaves.

The new law affected only slaves born before July 4, 1799. All younger ones had previously been "freed," although they had to remain as unpaid servants—the boys to the age of twenty-eight, and the girls to twenty-five. But now the older ones too were to be freed. Today? No, in ten years' time. By July 4, 1827, all slaveowners in New York State had to free every slave over twenty-eight years of age. But ten years—now, how long is that? A slave perhaps could mark the seasons on a stick or work them into a dance. Ten more plowings and plantings, ten more times to reap the wheat and pick the ripe apples, card the fall wool and slaughter the pig, pickle the meat and make the summer sausage. Ten more years of cooking and laundering and "yes, master," and "yes, missus," with never a "thank you." Ten more years—then what would be changed? Where would they go? What would they do?

Ten years. Dreams and doubts. All any slave could know for sure was that in ten years some would die and more would be born. Ten years is a long time to wait in uncertainty.

Still, as freedom drew nearer, it seemed to Belle and to every other slave more and more like distant drums beating, first very far away, then closer and closer, filling each man and woman with an irresistible excitement, a promise of new and different times. By contrast, slavery seemed uglier each day and harder to bear.

Slavery—that meant Mrs. Dumont.

Belle's baby was crying again. Mrs. Dumont seemed not to notice. Belle stopped rolling the biscuit dough. "Baby's cryin', missus. Have to tend to her now."

"Oh, stop worrying about your baby, Belle. She'll stop crying soon enough. Just get along with your work."

But Dumont's face was looking angrily through the door. "Wife, why do you not see the child is taken care of? I cannot bear to hear a child cry so. Belle, take care of the baby. I don't care if no more work is done for a week."

In the spring and summer months taking care of a baby was easier. Belle could sometimes leave the kitchen to Kate and Mrs. Dumont. There was work in the fields. The tiny, round infant fitted snugly inside a basket and Belle would hang it carefully from a branch near where she hoed or reaped. There was always a small child to keep the basket gently swinging while the baby slept peacefully on. As she worked Belle would croon a lullaby. And when she had finished her work, she would pick up the basket again by its rope and stride back through the fields, the baby quietly sleeping on.

Fall came. She had just finished quartering the apples and stringing them in the attic to dry. "Belle!" It was Kate shouting to her from below. Belle leaned out.

"Belle, master says your pa's dead. He just heard they're buryin' him this afternoon. If you want to see him, you better hurry."

Belle stood motionless, looking out over the fields. She re-

membered Ma-Ma's death. And she remembered the last time she
had seen Bomefree. It had been a beautiful summer day. She had
found him, almost by accident, seated by the road, far from any
house.

After Ma-Ma's death, the Hardenberghs had pretended to take
turns caring for the old man. He would be allowed to stay a few
weeks at one Hardenbergh house, then a few weeks at the next.
The day Belle had found him, he had been leaning on a rock,
resting between the last house and the one he was headed for,
twenty miles up the road. He had seemed to be looking directly at
her as the wagon approached, but until she spoke he had showed
no recognition. It was only then she had realized that, even in
broad daylight, he could no longer see her.

Belle and old Cato had pulled him up on the wagon seat and
driven him to his destination, the same damp cellar where she had
left him wailing from loneliness after Ma-Ma's burial. And again
the old man sobbed out his misery.

"All my children been taken away. Not one to bring an old
man a cup of water. What reason do I have to live?"

Listening to her father that day, Dumont's Belle desperately
wished Freedom Day was closer. "Just wait, Daddy," she had
begged. "It won't be so long before I'm free. Then I'll be able to
take care of you just like Ma-Ma used to."

But her words seemed only to make the old man's crying
worse. "I can't wait so long," he moaned.

Now she too was weeping. "Please, please, try, Daddy. Just try.
You'll see, I'll take such good care of you when I'm free."

Many years later, Bomefree's daughter said, "I truly thought, in
my ignorance, that he could live, if only he wanted to. I insisted he
could live. But he just kept shaking his head, insisting he could
not."

That was Belle's last sight of Bomefree alive.

Several years later she walked twelve miles hoping to see her father. That day she carried her second child, Peter, in her arms. She had wanted Bomefree to see his grandson at least once before he died. But when she came to the place where Bomefree had been staying, she found he had already crept up the road toward the next refuge. That day, she had had no time to follow.

After that Belle had only occasional news of her father. He was no longer staying with any member of the Hardenbergh family. They had grown tired of their own arrangement and had found another they preferred. Still pretending to satisfy the law that stated an old slave must not simply be abandoned, they had offered freedom to two other equally old slaves: Caesar, the brother of Ma-Ma, and his wife Betsy.

They were both too weak and old to even care for themselves properly. But now they were expected to feed, clothe, and somehow care for Bomefree. The three old people were given a one-room shack in the woods, far from any neighbor. Betsy was the first to die, and Caesar followed shortly after. Once again Bomefree was alone.

The day the old man was buried, Old Soan, who had been the last to see Bomefree alive, stood next to Belle at the graveside. She described passing by his shack only the week before. "He begged me to stay, Belle—moanin' so, it hurt me to hear him. 'Help me clean up,' he says. But I didn't dare stop. I felt so hungry and weak myself, Belle, I was scared I'd just fall down on top of him and never get up again."

A few days later a white man had found Bomefree dead. He reported finding no food or water in the hut. When the report reached them, the Hardenberghs shook their heads. The old Colonel's grandson was insistent, "If any slave of ours ever deserved a good funeral, Bomefree certainly does." And to prove his sincerity, he even attended the burial himself.

Belle noticed that the coffin had been painted black. That was something special. A slave coffin usually was only bare pine boards. And the Hardenberghs even had provided Bomefree's mourners with a jug of tasty applejack.

Barefooted, wearing a castoff gown of Mrs. Dumont's that was much too short for her, Belle walked behind the box that held her father's body. Her third child, "Dumont's Hannah," hung heavy on the young mother's hip, round fat fingers clutching at the frayed gown as Belle watched the black coffin lowered into a shallow hole in the uncared-for ground reserved for the bodies of the Hardenberghs' most faithful slaves.

Belle shifted Hannah's weight to her other arm. With every child she bore Belle found one more reason for wanting her freedom soon, while she was still young enough to try to make a better life. Somewhere, she felt it now with all her heart, there must be a better tomorrow for those of God's children born black.

A Slaveholder's Promise

EIGHT

&❧ Freedom Day in New York State was only two years away when Dumont sold Belle's son Peter. That is, he did not exactly sell Peter, since the boy, by law, had been born free. But Dumont, as the owner of the boy's mother, could sell his right to Peter's services until the boy should reach age twenty-eight. The boy was four at the time.

For the first time in her life, Belle openly opposed her master. Eyes wide with fear, she had planted herself squarely in front of Dumont.

"Master, don't send my boy away. What'll happen to him?

Maybe they'll beat him, and him such a little boy. Maybe they'll send him south and then he never be free. Please, please, don't sell my boy."

Dumont stared at her. "Belle, whatever has come over you? Solomon Gedney would never sell Peter south. You should know that. The law of this state forbids such a thing, and in any case, I would not permit it. Mr. Gedney is very taken with your boy. He wants Peter for himself. I should think you would be pleased to have him go into a nice home where he can be trained to work for a gentleman." He frowned at her, "Just stop worrying. Peter will be very happy with the Gedneys."

Belle stood silently as he walked away. She had never before challenged her master. Now she did not know what more to do. But she had not given up. As Freedom Day approached Dumont's obedient slave was rapidly changing. A new Belle was taking shape, and that Belle knew with certainty she would get Peter back some day. How? She did not know. But she would get him back.

Shortly afterward, Dumont made Belle a promise. She had been shucking peas in the kitchen when he walked in and stood watching her for a while. "Belle," he finally said. "You're the best worker I ever had. I've been thinking I'd like to give you a special reward. If you work extra hard over this next year I'll free you and Tom a full year before the law says I must. What's more, I'll let you have that cabin up the road to live in for as long as you and your family need it."

The summer had come and gone since then, and now the snow was starting to melt. But in all those months Belle had hardly rested a moment for fear she would not earn the reward Dumont had promised. At times, during that year, the slaves had seemed to mock her almost as much as they used to. "Master be crazy to give you up a year early." But she only shrugged off their laughter and exerted even more effort. The longing to be free and to have her children had taken deep root in Belle. She absolutely believed this to be the final year of her bondage—in spite of her accident.

The accident had happened just a short time after her master had given her his promise. A scythe, twisting in her grasp, cut deeply into her hand. Working with a sore hand had been painful and difficult. The wound kept reopening because she was so eager to get things done. She just could not give it time to heal properly. Nevertheless, looking back, she knew she had worked well and accomplished just as much as usual during that long year. It would only be a short time now to freedom.

Belle was sitting by the fire listening to the talk in the slave kitchen. Her fourth child, Elizabeth, leaned against Belle's knee, while the new baby, Sophia, sucked at her mother's breast. The talk was always the same now. Every slave in Ulster County was thinking and dreaming about nothing but Freedom Day. Even old Cato, though he would never admit it, was dreaming about that. Belle could hear the old preacher's cracked voice insisting, as it had for years, "All this freedom talk. Jus' another white folks' trick. Five masters Cato's had. Not one ever keep a promise."

Nero shook his head stubbornly. The scar made by a previous master's cane neatly divided his cheek in half. The younger man spoke slowly. "This white folks' promise gotta be different," he said. "It been made to every slave over twenty-eight in this state. Even master Dumont talk about freedom now, right out in front of us all. Master Dumont can't go back on that kind of talk. Too late. If he try—there be terrible trouble. Terrible trouble." As the stocky farmhand repeated the phrase, his face clouded and his hands became huge blunt fists. Then a slow, intent look replaced the look of anger on his face. "Besides," he said carefully, "no one's talkin' about any master's promise. This here's a law they made up in Albany. Even a master's got to obey a law."

"Some trick to it," Cato insisted. "Got to be some trick."

As she listened, there flashed into Belle's mind the face of the man she had met on the road so long ago. She had learned that his name was Levi Rowe. "It is not right thee should be a slave," he had said. Albany must be full of people like that, she thought. Today those people made laws that masters had to obey—even Dumont. As a matter of fact, Belle had increasingly come to doubt that Dumont could really be the Mighty Being. If he were, how could there be others in Albany with power over him?

Elizabeth was asleep, her head on Belle's knee; the baby, too, was sound asleep. Belle looked down at Sophia's peaceful round face with its tiny open mouth and at the tight pigtails poking out from the back of the older child's head. She crooned softly, "Your ma'll be free soon, little children. Freedom's coming soon now."

She looked up to find Nero still shaking his round head firmly. "Law says we go free. Next year, when time comes, no master stop me takin' my freedom." He stretched powerfully, drew back from the fire and lay down on his straw pallet to sleep.

Soon the room was full of slow, regular breathing. Only Belle remained awake, staring into the fire. She could easily distinguish Tom's wheeze in the far corner. Diana and Hannah were sleeping next to him. Dumont had promised to free her right after the holiday. It was only two more months to Pinxster. Belle could hardly wait.

But Pinxster came and went—and nothing more was said about freeing Belle. At last she could wait no more. She went up to Dumont. "Will you be giving me my free paper soon, master?"

Dumont's shaggy brows drew together sharply. "Come, now! Surely you know that last year was a bad year. The Hessian fly ruined the wheat again. I can't possibly afford to let you go. I need your help far too much."

She did not believe the words she had heard. "But you promised me."

"I said 'if you worked well.' Now you know as well as I that your hand has greatly interfered with your work in the past year."

She still was not willing to believe. "I worked so hard, master. I washed clothes and I scrubbed the pots and pans and I cooked and I reaped alongside the men. I did everything as usual, even with a bad hand. I let my children cry when they needed me. And only because you promised me my papers."

His voice grew curt, "Belle, don't worry. You'll get your freedom when the others get theirs. It only means another year. That's the best I can do."

Was it really only sixteen years ago that a frightened thirteen-year-old girl had stared up at a white face framed against the sky and wondered, "Is he kind?" It seemed three lifetimes away. For the first time since that day, Belle looked at John Dumont with neither fear nor gratitude.

Ma-Ma had said, "Never lie." And Belle had never lied. Yet her master thought nothing of lying to her. There he stood—with those same wide shoulders and the kindly face that had originally inspired such hope in Belle—showing no embarrassment at his broken promise. It was only a promise to a slave.

She never forgot that moment. For the first time she saw her master as just an ordinary slaveowner, very little better than the man who whipped his slave half to death.

Was it only the other day that she had scolded her hungry baby and then spanked it when it would not hush, because she would not take even one slice of bread from Dumont's cupboard without first asking? Yet he took her work, her son, everything from her—and never asked.

By the time she fell asleep that summer night in 1826, Dumont's Belle had reached a decision. For the first time in her life

Belle was going to take something without permission. She was certain of one thing: her freedom now belonged to her. She had earned it, just as surely as a free worker earns his wage. If Dumont would not give it to her willingly, she would take it as her due. And yet the habit of being fair to Dumont was so strong, Belle found even now she could not rid herself of that habit. Her master had often been kind. She would repay him. She would make quite sure all the fall work was done before she inconvenienced him by running away.

Once more the six-foot woman with the powerful body helped rake her master's hay and bind his wheat and smoke the hams after the fall slaughtering. Once more she worked overtime to help Mrs. Dumont stuff the summer sausage and store it in the bin where the oats would keep it from spoiling. Once more she cut hundreds of apples and pears into quarters and strung them high in the attic to dry. But her biggest job that fall was spinning the wool. It seemed to her the sheep had never before grown such thick fleeces. More than one hundred pounds came off their dirty woolly backs. She washed the wool and carded it and spun it onto long wooden spools. And somehow, at last, the work was done.

Now Belle could find time to be afraid. She had never before disobeyed her master. What would happen when she did? How could she get away safely? "God, I'm too scared to go at night, and if I go in the day, folks'll see me. What'll I do?"

Then an idea came: leave just before dawn. Day would follow soon enough, but an early start would give her plenty of time to leave the neighborhood before her absence was noticed.

"God," she prayed, kneeling for the last time on her praying ground. "That's a good thought. Thank you, God." Then Belle noticed a truly strange thing. It was the first time in a long while that she had prayed without imagining John Dumont's face up there in the sky.

It was still dark. The first rays were barely touching the ridges across the Hudson when Belle's lanky figure carefully stepped through the door and into Dumont's yard. She had told no one her plans, not even Tom. She could not risk being found out. On one arm she carried her baby Sophia. She knew that the other slaves would care for her older children. In a bright red kerchief was a bit of bread and summer sausage. The new Belle had decided she was entitled to that, too, without asking.

She strode barefoot at a fast lope down the road, away from those cliffs overlooking the Hudson. She was moving very fast indeed, but to her horror the day came even faster. At the top of a hill it dawned, full in her face, brighter than any day she could ever remember. She thought, "The day has no right to be so bright."

Where was she to hide? Like all slaves, Belle had never had reason to learn to plan ahead. So now it had not occurred to her to plan more than her actual departure.

While she puzzled, Belle decided to sit down to feed her infant. As the baby tugged greedily at her breast, Belle suddenly remembered the man who had stopped her on the road so many years ago. Levi Rowe lived nearby. "It is not right thee should be a slave," he had said. "God does not want it." Surely that man would help her now.

She found him at home, but so sick he could hardly find strength to speak. Nevertheless his smile and gesture made her feel welcome, as with great effort he managed to tell her of two places where she might find refuge and work. Before leaving, Belle straightened his bed for him as best she could, then thanked him, and hoisting her heavy baby once more in her arms, continued down the road.

As she came to the first house recommended by Levi Rowe, she recalled clearly having seen it before and remembered with even more pleasure the faces of its owners. "That's the place for me," she exclaimed. "I'll stop there." And she turned up the path toward the house.

The old woman who answered Belle's knock expressed no surprise at finding the tall black woman on her doorstep. "Will you come in and have cider and biscuits?" she said. "My children should be back very soon."

While Sophie gnawed contentedly on a biscuit, Belle perched shyly on a kitchen stool and waited. But not for long. Soon a wagon rumbled outside, and a man entered, followed immediately by a woman. They were the faces Belle had remembered.

"Rowe was right to direct thee here. We do have work for thee," the man said, adding sadly, "Old Rowe is so ill, I am afraid it may be his last good deed."

Impatient to prove her worth, Belle paid little attention to the second remark but picked up a broom and started whisking it energetically over the floor. She was thinking proudly that this was her first task as a free woman, when hooves were heard pounding on the road outside. Without even turning her head, Belle knew it must be Dumont.

To tell the truth, she had purposely not gone too far. She knew that Dumont would catch up with her and that the farther he had to travel the angrier he would be. Moreover she preferred not to leave Ulster County where her children were. Now that she had claimed it, she believed God somehow would make her master grant her the freedom she had earned.

But first she must face Dumont. He was blocking the kitchen door.

"Well, Belle. So you've run away from me."

"No, master, I did not run away. I walked away by day, 'cause you had promised me a year of my time."

"You'll have to come straight home with me."

"No, master." (Was it really she, Belle, speaking such words to Dumont?)

"I'll take the child."

"No, you'll not take my child."

Master and slave glared at each other, their silence filling the small room until a gentle voice behind Belle broke the tension. "I'm not in the habit of buying and selling slaves. Slavery's wrong and I'll have no part of it. But rather than have thee take the mother and child back, let me buy her services from thee for the rest of the year. She'll be lost to thee, in any case, come next July."

Dumont hesitated. Then he shrugged impatiently. After sixteen years it took him only thirty seconds to sell Belle. Twenty dollars for the mother's services for a year? Agreed. Five for the child's services until she is twenty-five? Agreed. And he left.

Belle lifted the broom again and turned toward her new owner. "Master. . . ."

The man held up his hand. "There is but one Master here. He who is thy Master is my Master."

Puzzled, she asked, "What should I call you then?"

"By my name," he replied. "Isaac Van Wagenen. And my wife is Maria Van Wagenen."

She looked down in wonder at their serene faces, her lanky body in its shabby slave-cloth dress towering over the two little Quakers. Then she turned back to work. They had bought her. Therefore, she belonged to them. But in her heart Belle knew it made no difference. Through her own struggle, she had won her freedom.

Sun Shinin' in a Pail

NINE

&~ "Come, Belle," said Mrs. Van Wagenen a little later. "Dinner is ready. Thee may sit here and eat with us."

It had been many years since Belle had eaten at a family table like a hired girl, not since she had lived with the Yankee Neelys. Eating at the master's table there had meant being forced to listen to Mrs. Neely's waspish whining at Mr. Neely. Belle would eat as fast and as quietly as she could, hoping to finish before Mrs. Neely turned on her.

This Quaker table was different. "Will thee please pass the butter, Isaac Van Wagenen?" "Belle, there is more milk in the kitchen. Please fetch it." "Please" was almost a new word in Belle's life. But like "thee" and "thou," it was a part of the Van Wagenens' ordinary speech. Their gentleness showed in everything they did. Belle thought, "I will be happy here."

But to her surprise, as the winter closed in along the length of the Hudson Valley, Belle found she was not happy.

"Sophie," she crooned to her baby. "What you suppose your sisters are doin'?" Sophie gurgled, while Belle shook her gently. "Gurgle and eat and sleep, that's all you do." She sighed, holding the small round shape up for a better look. "Why can't you grow fast like the wheat'll be growin' pretty soon? Can't you see your ma needs company?"

The late winter afternoons drifted slowly past, interrupted only by the low murmur of Isaac and Maria or the old mother reading the Bible. After the bustling activity of Dumont's slave kitchen, life at the Van Wagenens' seemed very dull indeed, lost in long stretches of contemplative silence.

Belle had a small room under the eaves for herself and Sophie. The straw pallet was clean and well stuffed. At first it had seemed exciting to have a room to herself. But soon it became just one more loneliness to endure.

The work of cleaning and cooking and tending the small vegetable garden and the chickens and the cow, in addition to keeping an eye on Sophie, kept Belle busy enough. But Isaac Van Wagenen had a small store in New Paltz where his wife helped out during the day, so there was only old Mrs. Van Wagenen left for company, and the gentle-faced old Quaker lady was less company than Sophie.

Belle sighed and hugged Sophie even more tightly. Her mind painted pictures of the slaves seated in front of the big fireplace at Dumont's. She could see their hands at work as they talked, deftly tying together dried rushes to make brooms or carving ladles out of birch wood. Ha! Now two of them were quarreling. But not so loudly as to risk Mrs. Dumont's poking in her head. The slave kitchen had not always proved a friendly place for Belle. She was too "different." She had expected, when she left home, to miss her family, but until now she never would have believed how much she would miss the movement and husky voices of the dark-skinned men and women that she was used to having around her. The worst of it was that here she did not even have the company of Ma-Ma's Mighty Being. She had always thought of God as someone to whom she could complain about a mean master or

This house, built by an Isaac Van Wagenen in Wagendahl near New Paltz, may be the one to which Belle fled from Dumont.

COURTESY NEW YORK PUBLIC LIBRARY

mistress. Where there were no complaints she could find no reason to talk to God.

So the weeks passed with Belle growing ever more homesick. She was always thinking of "home" and home was Dumont's. The slaves were sowing the grass seed and the clover now in the fields by the Hudson. They always did it while the snow was still on the ground. The sower's footprints in the snow guided him back and forth and helped him sow in straight lines across the field.

And now the snow had melted. The spongy ground around the Van Wagenen house squished underfoot. Tiny pale-green clumps of leaves poked out along the oak branches and along the bare, gray twigs of the bushes. Even the air smelled new.

Another month passed. Pink blossoms had broken out between the leaves of the mountain laurel. Belle could hardly bear it: it was time for Pinxster.

One Sunday she got up and determinedly informed the Van Wagenens, "My old master will come today, and I will return with him."

The Van Wagenens were astonished. "What makes thee suppose Dumont will come today?" they asked. "Who told thee such a tale?"

"No one told me," she replied calmly. "But I know he will come."

Later that afternoon, they heard the carriage pull in at the gate. It was Dumont. When Belle announced her intention to return, he smiled. "You ran away from me. What makes you suppose I would take you back now? If you suppose that, you are quite mistaken, for I will do no such thing."

But Belle studied only his smile, which seemed to contradict his words. She was sure the smile was his real answer. It seemed to be saying, "Come along then."

She went into her room, dressed her baby, and set out toward the gate where the carriage and horse waited for Dumont.

In later years, when telling about that day, she claimed she had been walking toward the gate when she suddenly felt an over-whelming force block her path, as if a powerful arm had been raised up to stop her. Some stern, invisible presence would not let her pass. She thought she distinctly heard a voice boom, "Not another step!"

She seemed to have no choice but to obey. In fact, she felt so dizzy she could not have advanced. Instead, she found herself forced slowly to turn and go back to her room, where she sat down, quite dazed.

And sitting in her small room she began to wonder, as if seeing herself for the first time: had she really been prepared to return to slavery of her own free will? Would she have left people who had treated her with respect and kindness to return to a master who had used her as a slave for sixteen years, sold her son, and in the end broken his solemn promise to free her? She realized that she would have returned. And as she explained later, "I felt so wicked when I saw this. I felt as if God would surely burn me up. And I cried, 'Oh, somebody, somebody, stand between God and me for it burns me.' And when I said this I felt as if something like an umbrella came between me and the light. I felt it was somebody —somebody that stood between me and God. And it felt cool, like a shade."

Timidly she asked, "Who's this that stands between me and God?" And then, more hopefully, "Is it old Cato?" But she seemed to see old Cato in the light and he was "all polluted and vile, like me." And she said "Is it Soan?" But she saw Soan in the light too, and she didn't look much better than Cato. Now Belle was getting impatient. "Who is this?" she asked.

"And then," she said later, "for a while it was like the sun shinin' in a pail of water when it moves up and down. I began to feel it was somebody that loved me, and I tried to know him. And

I said 'I know you! I know you! I know you!' And then I said, 'I
don't know you! I don't know you! I don't know you!' and when
I said 'I know you, I know you,' the light came. And when I said
'I don't know you, I don't know you,' the light went—just like the
sun in a pail of water. And finally something in me spoke up and
said, 'This is Jesus.' And I spoke out, with all my might, saying,
'This is Jesus! Glory be to God!' And the whole world grew bright
and the trees they waved and waved in glory, and every little bit
of stone on the ground shone like glass. And I shouted 'Praise,
praise, praise to the Lord.' And I began to feel such a love in my
soul as I never felt before—love to all creatures."

But as quickly as it had come, Belle's feeling of love vanished.
A dark thought had slipped into its place: "What about the white
folks that have abused you and beat you and abused your people
—think of them. Could you love them?"

It was a stern question, impossible to ignore. But then, she said
later: "There came another rush of love through my soul and I
cried out loud, 'Lord, Lord, I can love even the white folks'"

For a long time she walked around her room in a dream, murmuring "Jesus loves me. Jesus is my Jesus. He'll love me always. I
won't be lonely any more."

But with Belle's new love came a new fear. Everyone she had
ever cared for—Bob, Ma-Ma, Bomefree, her brother, her son, her
daughters—all had been taken away except baby Sophie. Now
she thought, "If I let white folks know about me and Jesus, maybe
they'll get him away from me too."

She could not risk that. Jesus was her secret friend. No one
must know he had come to her.

Many years later, when Sojourner Truth told this story, friends
asked her, "But Sojourner, where had you heard of Jesus?" She
replied, "Oh, I had heard his name many times. But I had always
thought of him as just an important person, like Washington and

Lafayette of whom there was much talk in the county in those days."

For a long time that afternoon, she sat quietly in her room, holding onto Sophie as tightly as if the baby herself were the new secret. At last she heard Maria call several times from below, "Belle, Belle. What can thee be doing up there?"

Belle walked slowly down, still clutching Sophie. Her face was somber. Maria looked at her oddly. "How strangely thee behaves today. Thee has lost thy chance to return to John Dumont. He would not wait for thee. Did thee change thy mind and not wish to return to him after all?"

"The Lord did not wish me to return and be a slave," Belle replied simply.

Maria's eyes studied her for a moment. "I am glad to hear it," she said finally. "Come, it is late. Let us prepare the supper."

I'll Have My Son

TEN

༄ July 4, 1827, the state of New York kept its promise and legally emancipated Isabelle Van Wagenen and all other slaves aged twenty-eight or more. There was no official public ceremony. Newspapers barely mentioned the occasion. Perhaps the editors felt there was no news in an event people had known was coming for ten years. But for Belle and most other New York State Negroes, July 4, 1827, was their first day as free Americans.

Isaac and Maria Van Wagenen smilingly conducted a small private ceremony in their home. Isaac read aloud from the Bible. Afterward, Maria kissed Belle on the cheek, handing her Sophie.

"Take thy Sophia, too, into freedom," she said. The earlier law gave them the right to keep the baby as an unpaid servant until she was twenty-five, but the Quakers wanted none of it. Then the three grownups sat down together and very formally bargained for Belle's wage. A tiny wage it was. A woman was never paid much, a black woman much less. But any wage Belle bargained for had the bright shine of her new freedom.

The next day seemed like any other day. Belle was still cooking, cleaning, washing, and ironing for Maria Van Wagenen and tripping over Sophie as the baby crawled about the house.

Even if the law had not allowed Dumont to keep her other daughters, Belle could not have made a home for them. Like any other servant, Belle had to "live in" wherever she happened to work. Old Tom could not help her. It was he who suffered most.

After Freedom Day, Dumont would not give Tom even a pallet for a bed. He was free now, and much worse, not useful. Belle's husband hobbled around town, doing odd jobs, sleeping where he could.

At least she could comfort herself that her daughters were in a safe place where they would be fed and surrounded by other black folk who knew them. That was a great deal to be thankful for. Meanwhile, for the first time she was free to look for her son.

Where was Peter? The boy seemed to have disappeared. He was no longer at Solomon Gedney's. When she had gone to look for him there, the black servants had looked nervously away. One day, she found an old woman, an ex-slave of the Gedneys', roaming the roads alone. That old woman had no reason not to tell Belle the truth.

Two hours later, Belle startled Mrs. Dumont by bursting unannounced into her kitchen. Mrs. Dumont spun around. "Belle," the familiar voice snapped like an icicle. "What do you mean, coming in like that?"

Belle had run all the way and could scarcely catch her breath to speak. But her bare feet were planted firmly on the wide planks of Mrs. Dumont's floor. Her former mistress's chilly disapproval had no power to frighten her.

"You sold my son," she said, trying to catch her breath. "But master promise he never be taken from the state. And the law say they can't take him. But now they give my son to Mr. Gedney's sister. Everyone knows she's married to Master Fowler and he lives in Alabama. They've taken my Peter south. Don't you know what that means? He'll never be free down there."

Her former mistress replied, "Ugh! A fine fuss to make about a little nigger. Why, haven't you as many of 'em left as you can see to? Making such a hallaballoo about the neighborhood, and all for a paltry nigger."

The tall dark woman in the shabby dress had been free a very short time. But looking down at the fashionably clothed body of that other who had tormented her for sixteen years, she said, feeling the truth in every word, "I'll have my child again."

"Have your child again!" repeated her mistress, her tone big with contempt. "How can you get him? And what have you to support him with if you could? Have you any money?"

"No," answered Belle. "I have no money, but God has enough. I'll have my child again."

Years later, remembering that day, she said, "When I spoke to my mistress that way, I felt so tall within. I felt as if the power of a nation was in me."

Now she went straight to Mrs. Gedney, the mother of Solomon and of Liza Fowler who had taken Peter south. Mrs. Gedney was quite as annoyed as Mrs. Dumont at the interruption, but she denied nothing. On the contrary. "Is your child better than my child?" she asked. "My child is gone out there, and yours is gone to live with her, to have enough of everything and be treated like a gentleman." And she began to laugh, a tinkly, bubbly laugh.

"Yes," said Belle. "Your child has gone there, but she is married and my boy has gone as a slave and he is too little to go so far from his mother."

But Mrs. Gedney could not stop laughing. "What a fuss to make about nothing," she gasped between giggles.

Outside, Belle sank down by the side of the road, holding her head between her worn, strong hands. What was she to do now? How could an ex-slave, a black woman who could not read or write, force white folks to take notice of their own law? Sitting there beside the road outside Mrs. Gedney's house, terrified and alone, Belle did not know what else to do but pray.

"God," she begged. "You just have to be my helper. Oh, please, show them that you are my helper."

And indeed if he did not show them, he did at least show her. For shortly after that, Belle met a man. She would never say, later, just who this man was. Abolitionists were unpopular in any Dutch county for many years after Freedom Day. She did not want to cause her friend trouble.

"The Quakers living over there are very angry about your son," this man said. "Why don't you go to them? I'm certain they'll help you and tell you what to do."

The man had pointed to a house nearby. A woman answered when Belle knocked. The woman apologized after hearing Belle's story. "It's late. Nothing can be done about this until morning. Will thee spend the night?"

She took Belle into a room where there was a great tall white bed. "Thee can sleep here," said the woman.

Belle said later, "I was kind of scared when she left me alone with that great white bed. I never had been in a real bed in my life. It never came into my mind she could mean me to sleep on it. So I just camped under it, and I slept pretty well there on the floor."

She was awakened next morning by the sound of the Quaker

woman's husband hitching up the horses. Belle and the whole family clambered into the wagon—mother, father, and seven children—and drove off. They left Belle just outside Kingston, giving her careful directions on how to get to the County courthouse and how to enter a complaint with the Grand Jury.

The wagon rolled off, leaving Belle alone again in the middle of the street. She stood for a moment, shivering with uncertainty. Then she pressed her lips firmly together and strode off, still keeping to the middle of the street. In fact, there was no other place to walk because of the great stacks of firewood piled in front of every house.

"Oh, God," she prayed, as she walked, "you know I've no money. Only you can make the people do for me. And you must make the people do for me, God. I'll never leave you alone 'til you do."

She already had forgotten the way to the courthouse and had to ask a passerby for directions. He pointed to a big building—the biggest she had ever seen—just up the street. Great square stone blocks were piled three stories high, with windows on the ground floor so tall a man could have walked through without stooping. A flight of stone steps led up to the door.

"Oh," she said later, "how small I did feel! Neither would you wonder, if you could have seen me, in my ignorance, trotting about the streets, meanly clad, bareheaded, and barefooted."

"Make the people hear me, God," she kept murmuring. "Don't let them turn me off without hearin' and helpin' me."

Men milled around like cows inside the great entrance hall. She noticed one that was dressed much grander than the others and immediately concluded that he must be the "Grand Jury." Belle walked over and started to tell him her story.

He listened a moment, then pointed up the stairs. "You'll have to go on up," he said.

Gripping the rail tightly (she was afraid that the people run-

ning up and down would roll her right back down like a ball),
Belle was shoving her way up the stairs when she spotted another
grand-looking man.

This one stopped with an expectant, amused air, as if he suspected that the strange-looking woman in front of him might be
worth a good laugh or two next time he wanted to amuse his
cronies. "What's your complaint?" he asked.

But when she told him, his manner quickly grew serious. "This
is no place to enter a complaint." He pointed up another, even
steeper flight. "The Grand Jury's sitting up there."

The room at the top of those stairs held a group of ordinary,
not at all grand-looking, white men. Most of them were seated on
small chairs lined up on one side, facing a tight-faced individual
who was boxed in behind a rail like a pig in a pen. Belle sailed
through the door. They looked up startled. Not waiting to be
asked, she told her story in her strong deep voice. A man hastily
led her out.

In the hall he asked, "Would you be willing to swear the
child you speak of is your son?"

She looked at him, surprised. "Oh, yes, I swear he is."

"Just a minute now. You'll have to make it official, and swear
by this book." He handed her one which she supposed later to
have been the Bible. She put it to her lips, as he instructed, and
began, once again, to swear Peter was her son.

This proved too much for several clerks standing nearby. Two
of them almost choked with laugher. "Lawyer Chip," one of these
asked, "what's the use of making her swear? She can't understand
what it means."

"It will answer the law," replied Lawyer Chip calmly. He sat
down and filled out a form. "Here." He handed the piece of paper
in his hand to Belle. "Take this writ back to New Paltz and give it
to the constable. He'll serve it on Solomon Gedney and make

Gedney get your son back to you."

She sped down the stairs—one flight, two flights, three. Out the open door she flew, the precious paper clutched in one hand. It was nine miles to New Paltz. No matter; she ran all the way. There she found the constable and handed him the writ.

But the constable made a mistake. Instead of serving the writ on Solomon Gedney, he served it on Solomon's brother. The constable was already home again before he realized his error. And while he was still scratching his head, wondering what to do, Solomon, who had been warned by his brothers, had slipped into a boat and was halfway across the Hudson. Solomon, however, knew the law. He knew he had to get the boy back. If he did not, he could be sentenced to fourteen years in prison or forced to pay a huge fine for selling a slave out of New York.

That year, 1827, there were no trains running up along the Hudson and westward to the Mississippi. Solomon Gedney had to sail down the river to New York, take a packet ship along the eastern coast of the United States, around Florida, through the Gulf of Mexico, and so to Mobile, Alabama.

He left in the fall of the year. Months passed. In the spring, Belle heard he had returned with Peter. She went to the Gedney house to claim her son. Solomon Gedney had only four words for her. "The boy is mine," he said.

And he slammed the door in her face.

Southern Scars

E L E V E N

𝆕 She thought a long time before doing anything further. She was afraid that if she made more trouble for him, Gedney might take it out on Peter. But Belle wanted her son. The law had been strong enough to force the white man to bring Peter back from the South. Because Gedney had broken the law, Peter legally was free. But who would force Gedney to return Peter to his mother? She went again to see Lawyer Chip.

The lawyer barely looked up from his papers.

"Lawyer Chip, Mr. Gedney won't give me back my son."

"The constable still has the writ, hasn't he? Just ask him to serve it again. But, this time, make sure he gets the right man."

A few days later Solomon Gedney galloped into Kingston on his chestnut mare, posted a six-hundred-dollar bond and promised to appear in court when called. People said they had never seen him look so angry. He was usually an affable man; but that day he said good morning to no one.

"Now, then, my good woman," said Lawyer Chip briskly, when Belle returned to him a fourth time for advice. "That's all we can do until next session. The court is adjourned for the season. But don't worry about it. You'll not have to wait more than a few months more."

"A few months?" She looked at the lawyer in dismay. "But that will give Master Gedney time to be off again with my child. And this time I might never catch up with him. No, no, I can't wait. I *must* have my child."

The lawyer rested the feather of his goosequill pen lightly alongside his long nose and winked slyly. "Just remember," he said, "if Gedney does remove the boy again, he'll stand to lose his six-hundred-dollar bond." He smiled at her. "One half of that money then will be yours."

He nodded pleasantly as if to say good-bye, and turned back to his papers.

A long moment passed. Without looking up, Lawyer Chip realized that the woman had not left. What on earth did she want? He put down his pen and stared at her, tapping his finger impatiently on the desk.

"I don't want money," she said in her deep voice. "I want my son. God will help me get him, I know, and not make me wait for next session."

The lawyer thought, "The woman is becoming insufferable. I should never have gotten myself involved in this." Aloud he said, "You realize, of course, that you ought to be mighty thankful for all we have already done. You've put us to a great deal of trouble. The least you can do now is to be reasonable and wait as I tell you to."

She saw, all too clearly, that there was no use staying any longer; he was tired of her.

She stepped out into the streets of Kingston. The stars were already out and she could see it would soon be dark. She wandered the roads a long time, wondering what to do. Try as she might she could think of no one in Kingston to help her now.

"God," she cried suddenly, extending her arms to the sky. "Are you tired of me, too?" Then she remembered Jesus. God might be tired of her but surely he would listen to Jesus. And she began to pray to Jesus to take up her case before God.

"Hallo, there."

A man stood across the road from her, smiling as if he knew her. Yet she was certain she had never seen him before.

"How are you doing with your boy? Are they giving him back to you?"

She told him of her difficulties, noticing at first how gentle his eyes were. But before she had finished, angry little lights had appeared in them, like sparks from a blacksmith's anvil.

"Now everybody is tired of me," she concluded. "There is no one left to help."

He folded his arms firmly on his chest. "All right now," he said. "Just listen to me, and I'll tell you what to do." He pointed across the street. "Do you see that stone house over yonder?" She nodded. "Lawyer Romeyne lives there. Go see him and tell him about your case. If I know him, he'll want to help you."

She was already moving up the road, with her long, swinging stride, when she heard the man call after her, "Now be sure to do what I say—stick to him. Don't give him any peace until he agrees to help you. If you press him hard enough, I have no doubt he'll do what he can."

Lawyer Romeyne was accustomed to meeting all kinds of people. But he barely could hide his surprise at the sight of the shabbily dressed, bare-footed giant of a woman whose deep voice now filled his small office. That big voice, he thought, would have been an asset to any lawyer pleading a case in court. She spoke with her own strange twists of phrase, including God in her story as if he were a man walking by her side. But her story had the ring of truth. "These are certainly new times," thought Lawyer Romeyne.

The young lawyer was a local man, just starting to practice. Up to now he had had few clients; to take on this one might drive away some prospective clients. But he was a man who believed strongly that laws were made to be observed. And there was no question whatever that the woman standing in front of him had a case.

"If you can bring me five dollars to pay a constable," he said, "I'll get your son back to you within twenty-four hours."

She turned up her empty hands. He nodded understandingly. "If you will go back to the same Quakers who carried you to court, I have no doubt that they can find you five dollars. Within twenty-four hours after you turn the money over to me, you will have your son back."

Her Quaker friends insisted on giving her more than five dollars. Belle turned the entire sum over to Romeyne. Afterward, people asked her why she had done this. "You're a fool," they said, meaning it kindly enough. "Look at your feet. You could at least have bought yourself a pair of shoes with the rest of the money."

She shook her head. "I do not need money or clothes now. I want my son. If five dollars will get him, more will surely get him even faster."

Romeyne had told her to return in twenty-four hours, he would have Peter back by then. But Belle had no way of counting time. In her impatience, she returned to the lawyer's office to check.

"Lawyer Romeyne, that woman's here again." It was the voice of Romeyne's servant. Belle stopped timidly in the hall. Was she becoming a nuisance? Would Romeyne grow weary of her too? But Romeyne's face appeared smiling in the door.

"Come back in the morning, and you will find your son here."

At dawn the great knocker on Romeyne's door came down again with a crash that sounded up and down the street. His servant stumbled to the door in her nightcap, yawning and irritable. "Squire Romeyne says to tell you the morning will not be with us until the sun is straight above. Your son will surely be here by noon. He has sent Matty Styles after him and Matty never yet has failed to bring back his man, dead or alive.

"Squire Romeyne says, too," the servant had to scream after Belle who already was halfway down the street. "He says to tell you you need not come again. He will send for you himself when the boy arrives."

How the morning dragged! The shadows of trees sprawled on the ground like the bodies of exhausted men. Belle thought those shadows would never have the strength to gather themselves together. But somehow, at last, there they were, all bunched under the trees, and it was noon. From where she sat she could see Romeyne walking toward her. He was frowning.

"Belle, I've seen your son. He says he has no mother or any other relative living around here. I'm afraid you'll have to come to the courthouse and identify him yourself."

Shaken by this unexpected news, Belle walked with Romeyne into the judge's chamber. She was met at the door by a scream that struck her like a brick in the face. Peter had seen his mother and had thrown himself to the floor, locking his arms around Solomon Gedney's knees. She could not believe that the words she heard were really coming from her son's mouth. "My master is so good to me. Oh, please, please don't take me away from him. Please, please, please. . . ."

Peter was trembling as hard as she. But Romeyne appeared to pay no attention. Walking over, he touched the boy's arm.

"What is that scar on your forehead, boy?" he asked.

Peter's enormous eyes remained fastened on his master's face. "Fowler's horse kicked me," he said in a whisper that could scarcely be heard.

"Speak up, boy," said Romeyne. "And the scar on your cheek?"

"I ran against the carriage." Peter was whimpering again, his arms still locked around Solomon Gedney's knees.

The judge interrupted. "Forget your master now, boy, and pay attention."

But Peter would not loosen his grip. "No, no," he kept insisting. "She's not my mother. My mother doesn't live in this town."

Belle's heart, under her faded calico gown, felt as tight as a pineknot. She watched the judge tapping his fingertips thoughtfully together. At last, he turned to her.

"Do you claim this is your boy?"

She nodded. She could not find a word to say. But Romeyne stepped forward hastily to speak for her. She hardly listened. Would she get her son back? And if she did? Already within the space of a few months, she had made so many enemies. The Gedneys were important people in those parts. What would they not do to get even with her? Would she be able to keep Peter and raise him?

The judge was speaking again. "I order that the boy be delivered into the hands of the mother, having no other master, no other controller, no other conductor but his mother."

Peter's terrified screams filled the room. It took Romeyne, the court clerks, and Belle, all working together, to quiet him. At last, his face streaked with tears, sucking on a piece of rock candy, he stared at Belle, and in a shy whisper, admitted, "You do look like my mother used to."

She took him to the house in Kingston where she had been working while waiting for the case to reach the court. She lifted his shirt over his head.

"Pete," she gasped. From his bony neck to his skinny thighs, scars and welts rose up side by side like fingers on a hand.

"That's where Master Fowler whipped and kicked and beat me," he said. He did not whimper at the memory.

"Oh, Lord Jesus, look! See my poor child!" cried Belle. And doubling her fists in grief and anger, she cried out, "Oh, Lord, render unto them double for what they have done."

It was a while before she could bring herself to speak again. "What did Miss Liza say, Pete, when you were treated so?"

"Oh, Ma, she said she wished I was with Belle. Sometimes I crawled under the stoop to hide, the blood runnin' all over me and my back stickin' to the boards. And sometimes Miss Liza would come and grease my sores when everyone was asleep."

"Was that why you wouldn't say you knew me, Pete? Were you scared Gedney would punish you more?"

"He said he would give me the wors' beatin' I ever had, if I didn't say what he wanted me to."

That night, as she lay awake next to Pete, Belle found herself wondering again about the man she had met on the road—who had directed her to Romeyne. The more now she tried to remember his face, the more she became convinced it must have been Jesus. Jesus had been standing by watching over her all that time, she thought. How else, she asked herself, could a penniless black woman who could not read or write have won such a battle against the slaveowners?

Turning over with a sigh, Belle curved an arm around Peter. Under the soft underside of her arm she felt again the rough welts rising along his back. And again she murmured, "Oh, Lord, render unto them double."

Changing Times

T W E L V E

ॐ Belle wasted no time finding Peter a job. "Turn my back—a sparrow wouldn't find time to wink an eye, but my Pete's already in trouble," she complained to Maria Van Wagenen.

Fortunately, there were some locks on Rondout Creek, not far from where the Van Wagenens lived. Locks were used to raise the water level of the creek so sloops and grain barges could pass to pick up wheat and other produce farther upstream. Soon Pete was living with the burly white man in charge, running errands and helping turn the great wheel that opened and closed the locks.

Meanwhile Sophie was living at Dumont's with her sisters.

Belle had found it impossible to care for the baby while working around Kingston and waiting for Pete's case to come up in court. Dumont long since had forgiven his former slave for running away, and unlike his wife, he felt guilty about Pete. He had been willing to let Sophie stay at his place where her sisters could watch over her while Belle was away. When Belle came back from Kingston, she found Dumont pleased enough with the arrangement, and the toddler was so happy there that she decided to leave her.

During the winter, the tall, rawboned woman worked around in several different homes. She was well-known in the county by now and had little trouble finding employment. One day, on her way to visit her children at Dumont's, she was stopped by a cousin of Solomon Gedney's who had called her the "worst of devils" at the trial but now offered her a temporary job taking care of several sick members of his family. She accepted the job, glad to do her part to heal bad feelings.

She had not been long at Gedney's cousin's house; she was standing in the yard trying to hang out some wet sheets and fighting the brisk wind that kept threatening to tear them from her hands, when a piercing shriek rang through the yard. Belle turned, hands clinging to the clothesline. With so much wind it was hard to be sure, but the shriek had seemed to come from the window upstairs. Now the kitchen door burst open, held by the force of the gale. The young daughter of the house stood before Belle. The child's face was the color of the wet sheets, her eyes dilated with terror.

"Oh, Belle," she whispered, "Fowler's murdered Aunt Liza." Whimpering with fright, she wrapped her arms around the tall black woman's waist and tried to bury her face in Belle's stomach.

Belle gently freed herself. She raced up the stairs, two at a time. She could hear voices coming through a closed door. Standing in the hall, she planted her ear carefully against the door. Gedney's cousin seemed to be reading aloud from a letter. She heard him say, "How long Fowler had been insane, we don't know. Nor what she had had to suffer at his hands before. But now her poor body lay on the floor, the blood pouring from the terrible wounds he had inflicted. It took three men to master him. He's locked up now and will be for the rest of his unhappy life, where he can do no more harm. As for the children, poor things, they are being sent north to live with Liza's parents."

In the hall outside, Belle lowered her face slowly into her hands. "Oh, God," she asked, "was it because I prayed that you 'render unto them double'? Oh, God, I did not mean quite so much." She found herself sobbing uncontrollably.

Every time Belle visited her daughters now, she noticed that there were fewer workers on the old place. "Lots of colored folk moving on," Nero remarked to her on one occasion. The short sturdy man with the scarred face was one of the few slaves Dumont had retained as a hired hand. "Now he has to pay us, seems Master Dumont don't need as much help as he used to. Too many now with no job, no home, no land. Folks are movin' out of the county. They've got to find work somewhere."

Nero motioned up the road with his thumb. "Up at Catlin's, same story. He's got both his own sons out there now, hoein' and rakin'. Those white boys never raised a finger to do a lick of work before in their life. I hear one of 'em took real sick." He spat neatly out the door. "Work's killin' him, I guess."

"Where's old Cato?" Belle asked.

"Don't know too well. But his four sons all headed up the Big Ditch couple of months ago. They say lots of jobs up that way."

Belle nodded. Many ex-slaves were joining the stream of settlers pouring through the Big Ditch, the new Erie Canal into western New York. Cities were sprouting up along the entire length of the Erie: Rochester, Buffalo, Syracuse. There were forests to clear up that way, wilderness to plow and plant, new factories rising on river banks that only Indian canoes had touched ten years ago. Yes, folks said there were plenty of jobs.

"Soan's daughter and her husband went downriver to New York," Belle said.

Nero scratched his scar, thoughtfully. "Most of 'em headin' that way. Wouldn't mind seein' New York myself."

From where Belle sat, leaves hid the Hudson from view. But she did not need to see the water to let her thoughts begin to drift, like a dry stick caught in the river's current. All her life, New York had stood there out of her sight, at the river mouth, drawing escaped slaves into its mysterious, crowded alleys. What strange tales those fugitives used to tell when they were captured and returned to their masters.

Year after year she had watched the tall masts and billowing sails of the great sloops passing the steep cliffs below Dumont's. On a summer's day like today, the sails dotted the river for miles. Newer boats passed, too, belching smoke and sparks, their enormous side-wheels churning the river to froth as white as the foam on Martin Schryver's beer. Folks claimed the new boats took only a single night to reach New York.

But most ex-slaves still traveled on foot as the fugitives had long ago. The route had not changed much. It was still a rough eighty miles of muddy cattle tracks and ruts cut by the wooden wheels of stage coaches and ox carts. Where there were bogs even the dirt track disappeared, leaving only slippery rotting logs over which laden vehicles lurched, splattering all they passed.

Nero said, "Why don't you go to New York, Belle? They say the city's growin' like a honeysuckle vine. One man tellin' me only the other day, he says a strong-lookin' black woman can't walk down the street in that city without some lady poppin' out the door to hire her. They say folks there pay twice what you get here."

"What about my children?" asked Belle.

"You're not livin' with them now," he pointed out. "Ain't they all right here?"

Belle shook her head. "I have to watch after Pete. He'd just get into more trouble in the city. And I'd worry about my girls. When the Lord is ready for me to go, he'll give me the sign."

The sun was already setting that day when she left to return to the Van Wagenen's. Soon only the stars lighted her road. As she passed a cluster of houses she noticed a frame building glowing in the dark. She knew it as a religious meeting place, though she had never attended any meetings there. She had never attended any church, in fact. Negroes were not generally welcomed. But this building belonged to a new church in the community, one that frequently held special meetings to attract new members. She had heard that anyone could attend these meetings and speak about their religious experiences. Yet she was hesitant to accept the invitation—she knew that "anyone" usually meant only white folk.

Now, creeping close, she peered in through a window. She saw not a single colored face. She did not dare go inside for fear that people would drive her away. But she could listen.

The meeting lasted several hours. Belle stood outside until the very end. Only when the people began to shift in their pews and the men to look for their hats, did she give herself a little shake, straighten up, and quickly walk on. As she strode down the moonlit road to the Van Wagenen's house, Belle kept wondering, "How can white folk be so much like me?"

While she had watched through the church window, a man had risen to his feet. At first he had been shy. His eyes looked nervously at the people around him, then dropped sheepishly to the floor. But as he talked he had seemed to take on courage. Belle soon realized in amazement that he was talking about her Jesus. He, too, had felt Jesus' presence. He had told how he used to beat his wife. But one day an unseen force had come, like a stern master, holding back his arm so that he could not strike the next blow. And then, as he stood trembling, a spirit of love suddenly had entered his heart as if from nowhere, and he had known that it was Jesus. "Jesus had come to be with me always," he said.

Belle could hardly believe her ears. A white man using her words to talk about Jesus. Why, she had been so afraid the white folks would get him away that she had kept her experience a secret even from her daughters.

By the end of the meeting at least a dozen people had risen to recite similar experiences, while the cries and the hallelujahs grew louder. And it began to appear to Belle that everyone there, at one time or another, had known her Jesus.

At first this thought frightened Belle. Could her Jesus be as big as the whole world, big enough to share with every man? If they all knew him, it could only mean he was, indeed, big enough. As she wrestled with these new thoughts, the voice of the congregation had come through the window, raised in a hymn whose words seemed to soar toward the stars—a song of hope, she thought, for all poor folk.

> *There is a holy city*
> *A world of light above*
> *Above the starry regions,*
> *Built by the God of Love.*

(The singing had started slowly.)

The meanest child of glory
Out shines the radiant sun,
But who can speak the splendor
Of Jesus on his throne.

(Soon, every voice was raised, while Belle hummed along, wishing she knew the words.)

Who speak of fiery trials
And tortures on their way
They come from tribulation
To everlasting day.

("Yes," she thought, "everlasting day!")

And what shall be my journey
How long I'll stay below,
Or what shall be my trials,
Are not for me to know.

As she walked away down the dark road, she resolved to try to join that church. They could not do worse than refuse her.

The next week, she screwed up her courage and presented herself—and to her surprise was accepted into what she soon learned was a Methodist church.

It was in this Methodist church that Belle met Miss Geer, a New York schoolteacher who took a great shine to Belle and to Peter. Very early in their acquaintance, this lady startled Belle by offering to take both Belle and Peter to New York.

"I'll be going back to the city in the fall," said Miss Geer. "If you and Peter care to accompany me, I'll be glad to pay your passage. A good worker like you, Belle, will find it easy to get a job. In fact, I have friends who would be delighted to hire you and at twice the wage you get here in Ulster County."

But the important thing, as Miss Geer pointed out, was that Peter would be able to go to school in the city. "It's a shame to waste a boy that smart up here where there aren't any schools for colored children. I'd be willing to pay his tuition in New York, myself, and make sure he gets an education. You don't want him tending locks for the rest of his life, do you, Belle?"

It was such a new idea, it took a while for Belle to get used to it. But of course she would love to have Peter go to school. And with a better wage she might even be able to save enough money to buy the house she had dreamed of for her children. The more she worked it over in her mind, the more Belle liked the plan. Finally all was decided; Belle and Pete would go to New York.

She spent a sad afternoon saying good-bye to the girls. "It'll only be a little while," she assured them, crying a bit as she hugged them. "You'll join me soon." She hadn't had time to go see old Tom. The county had finally taken pity on him and lodged him in the county poorhouse, many miles away.

Sometime during the late summer of 1829, Isabelle Van Wagenen thrust her extra black dress and the spare pants she had made for Peter into a pillow case. She tied a white bandanna on her head and laced up the shoes the cobbler had made for her. It was the first new pair she had ever had. Before, when she had had any shoes, they had always been men's castoffs; her feet were too large for any mistress's hand-me-downs. Now, clutching Peter tightly by the hand and accompanied by Miss Geer, Belle boarded a sloop for New York.

God in the City

THIRTEEN

ಶಿ Big boats, little boats, sloops, packets, steamboats, and sail-
boats. Masts rose into the twilight sky like a forest of naked
birches, hemming in the great, gray city. Behind the masts, squat
buildings packed the lower part of Manhattan like a flock of dirty
sheep crowding into a pen. She imagined those in front bracing
their toes to keep from being shoved into the river by those behind. Up and down the riverbank the buildings stretched in a
low, unbroken line, while beyond, slender wooden church spires
shot toward heaven, like willow shoots sprouting after a warm
spring rain. Belle felt better seeing those spires. So many of them

A busy dock at South Street and Maiden Lane, New York City, where most Hudson River boats landed in 1828. (The Edward W. C. Arnold Collection, lent by the Metropolitan Museum of Art.)
COURTESY MUSEUM OF THE CITY OF NEW YORK

Traffic flying past Belle's coach in 1829 must have looked much like this Broadway scene drawn two years later.
COURTESY MUSEUM OF THE CITY OF NEW YORK

in evidence must surely be a sign that God was closer to man here than in Ulster County.

An energetic young boy with stringy muscular legs darted off to find the new arrivals a carriage. Miss Geer clutched her carpet-bag, nervously waiting, but he was quickly back with a carriage, seated next to the driver. The schoolteacher sighed with relief.

"We're lucky to get any carriage," she said, as they scrambled in. "This port's been growing so fast since the Erie Canal opened —they do say we've as many people now as Boston or Philadelphia. Can't build fast enough to fit 'em all in."

Their carriage rolled out from the smelly slip, over a road littered with rotting produce and cluttered with bales and boxes. A troop of pigs ran squealing out of their path, then stopped to root in garbage by the road.

Belle wrinkled her nose. Pigs aplenty they had in Ulster County but no town as untidy as this. She thought it strange to see merchants doing business on walks alongside the road, while carpenters sawed and banged away and pedestrians picked their way past as if such disorder were a matter of course. Over there, a building was going up. Over here, one was coming down. Everything seemed to be doing a crazy dance all its own.

Their carriage had turned and was rolling along a broad, straight avenue paved with round stones. "Broadway," announced Miss Geer, importantly. "Cobblestones," she added, pointing down with her little finger. To Belle the crowd scurrying along the wide walks seemed enormous. Heavy, bright-colored signs dangled from above, close to their bobbing heads."

The carriage rumbled on . . . an omnibus clanged past, pulled by perspiring horses . . . a heavily laden cart lurched along, narrowly missing three pedestrians . . . two carts locked wheels . . . a whip swished across a horse's back . . . a driver cursed . . . .

Belle sat as stiff as an oak branch, her arm tight around Peter.

She was glad for the protection of the carriage sides and was already longing for the quiet places she had left—neat, blue lime-stone houses, huge stone barns into which cows drifted at milking time, peaceful streets blocked only with piles of clean, dry fire-wood. The noise and violence here repelled her.

She felt better when the carriage turned into a side street. The narrow vertical houses were taller than those back home, but she liked the pretty red brick with its white seams and the neatly painted wooden houses. She was relieved to see the horses stop before one of these. Miss Geer leaned forward. "My friends are expecting us," she said.

And so by morning Belle was at work as if she had never left Ulster County—scrubbing the collars of a master's shirt, heating a flatiron over a wood fire, whisking a rush broom over wide plank floors, running upstairs to plump the soft feather mattress where a mistress had slept. Cooking, cleaning, washing.

It was familiar work. Only the place and the faces of her new employers were different. And soon these, too, were familiar, and even the noises of the city startled Belle no more than the lowing of a cow or the "ratatat" of a woodpecker.

She became accustomed to hearing English spoken everywhere around her and to speaking it herself. She had picked up English at the Dumonts', where Mrs. Dumont preferred it. And it had been the only language spoken among her Methodist friends in Ulster County, although she, herself, always spoke with a heavy Dutch accent, as did many New York State Negroes.

She learned very soon now not to jump when the great BOOM sounded over the harbor just before dawn. It was only the gun at Governor's Island saluting the sun. And the strange, hoarse cry she heard that first morning, as she was starting the fire—"Sweep, O-O-O-O-O-O-O. Sweep, O-O-O-O-O-O-O." That was the chimney sweep—a scrawny Negro boy, smaller than Peter— carrying a long-handled broom. Two dull, dirt-rimmed eyes had turned up to her for a moment, just time enough for her to glimpse the pinched, soot-stained face under the soiled stocking cap. An old man's face on a gaunt, hungry little boy.

She learned to recognize the peddlers' sing-song cries and know which carts to hail. The cattail vender clop-clopped his horse rapidly by, cart piled high with tall tufted reeds plucked from Long Island marshes. He never stopped on Belle's street. He would sell his cattails in the Five Points area where the very poorest people lived, and they would use them to stuff the pallets on which they slept. The straw peddler walked his horse more slowly, turning his head right and left. He might make a sale here. Straw frequently was used to pad a servant's bed.

In the fall, Belle learned the cry of the sandman, his cart loaded with gleaming particles from beaches she had never seen. "Here's white sand. Choice sand. Here's your lily white sand. Here's your Rockaway Beach sand." Sand sprinkled on a city floor kept it dry and clean in winter.

The vegetable man had one cry, the strawberry girl another. City dogs barked as loudly as country dogs. The scavenging pigs oinked along the street. Horses whinnied impatiently. It was not, after all, so difficult to get used to the sounds of a big city.

At first, life was much as Belle had hoped it would be. Every month she dropped half her big-city pay into a purse she kept in a pocket carefully sewn into the straw pallet on which she slept. She was saving for that home she hoped to buy for her children some day. And Peter was in school.

As she had promised, Miss Geer arranged for Peter to enter a navigation school and paid his tuition. Not only was he learning to read and write; some day Pete would be ready to work as a pilot on a boat. The future seemed to hold all the promise the slave Belle had once imagined to be contained in that simple word "freedom."

But the problem that had seemed easiest to solve, when she was looking at all those spires rising above the harbor like God's finger reminding man of justice, turned out to be the most difficult. Belle could not find a church to attend.

She had first chosen the leading Methodist church of New York City. Arriving at the door one Sunday, neatly clad in her heavy new shoes and a severe black gown, she had handed the elder standing there a letter of introduction from her church in Ulster County. He had read it politely and said, "Will you be so kind as to return in the afternoon when the colored class meets?"

No, she would not attend a segregated church, she told him. She tried several more churches and finally had to settle for one run by Negroes for Negroes. The founders were people who had grown tired of sitting in the "colored class" of a white church. Their church was segregated too, of course, but not because her people chose to have it so. White folks were welcome in the black church, but they never came. Belle wondered whether there was any place in all that town where black could worship with white.

One day Miss Geer invited Belle to join an evangelist group to which she belonged. They were street missionaries who struggled enthusiastically to bring religion to the poor. "You know, Belle," said Miss Geer earnestly, "If we could just make the poor believe in Jesus and obey his laws, we could rid the city of all the crime and misery that fill its streets.

"Why don't you come with us?" the elderly school teacher urged. "Our street meetings may turn out to be exactly what you've been seeking. And you can be so useful to us. Your height and your singing will attract new people, and with your dark skin you can walk in safety where we would never dare set foot." Miss Geer was beginning to get quite excited at the prospect. "Why, you could go right into the Old Brewery tenement building and other awful places and invite people out to hear us preach. Why not join us next Sunday and see how things go?"

Belle quickly decided that Miss Geer's invitation might well be that sign from the Lord she had been expecting. She had been trying to find a way to worship her Lord in church. Perhaps he had been turning her away from church after church because he needed her to work in the street, to spread his gospel among the poor.

Next Sunday afternoon, Belle stationed herself on a corner of the Lower Bowery, eyes closed, low voice sending the notes of her hymn soaring between the dirty, gray walls of the tumble-down buildings around her.

It was early in the morning,
It was early in the morning,
Just at the break of day
When he rose, when he rose,
And went to heaven on a cloud.

In that day, the very poorest of New York's people lived along the lower Bowery in an area known as Five Points, near where the city's Chinatown stands today. The area formerly had been a swamp. Horrible odors used to come from it and squadrons of mosquitoes and flies used it as a safe base from which to invade the city. At last, local citizens forced the city fathers to drain the land. But the work was done too hastily; the houses were still new when they began to tip and sink into the soft ground. The rich quickly found homes elsewhere, and the poor drifted into the empty, unwanted buildings.

By the time Belle turned her feet into Five Points' dark, narrow ways, seeking souls for Miss Geer's meetings, the crumbling tenements sheltered thousands of penniless Irish immigrants and Negroes. The mud in the alleys oozed over the tops of Belle's shoes. Swollen faces stared curiously at her through broken windows. She stumbled up pitch-dark stairs, clutching at broken railings, losing her footing where a step was missing.

"It was early in the morning, it was early in the morning . . ." She would be singing almost to herself as she walked the dark, dirty ways, trying to keep up her courage.

Belle would never forget the scenes of human suffering she saw in the Five Points. The people seemed far worse off than the rural slaves she had known back in Ulster County. Door after door opened to reveal men, women, and children lying listlessly on filthy pallets or seated on empty boxes, staring with unseeing eyes. One group was sleeping, cramped so close around a small fire that their heads or feet almost touched the burning coals. The sharp smell of their singed clothing brought tears to her eyes. Belle was never surprised that so few people could be led from Five Points to attend Miss Geer's meetings. There was no hope left in those tenements; the people were too tired, too weak from despair and hunger.

But occasionally, on the outskirts of the district, Miss Geer would discover groups of women who seemed rather better off. They usually lived all together in a single house, and were often delighted to let the lady missionaries in. One day, in a room filled with over-stuffed furniture, Belle opened one such meeting:

> *There is a holy city*
> *A world of light above,*
> *Above the starry regions,*
> *Built by the God of love.*

Miss Geer began to speak, urging their listeners to give up sin and seek the way of righteousness. The listening women seemed unusually receptive. One after the other rose to her feet, and with cries and groans and moaning and swaying, began to confess to a procession of sins. Belle had never heard such wild talk, nor observed such behavior. One pretty woman, her long black hair streaming down her back, grew so excited, she soon was running around in a circle, barking like a dog. Another, in a bright green dress, for no apparent reason that Belle could see, suddenly leaped into the air with a piercing shriek, then fainted in a graceful heap on the floor. Several young women began foaming at the mouth. Others wept.

If Jesus had been present when all this started, Belle was certain he must have moved quietly on by this time just as she would have liked to do. She was noticing that Miss Geer also appeared a little put out when suddenly Belle felt a tremendous yank on her skirt that pitched her to the floor and a plump female landed on top of her. The woman had caught her foot in the hem of Belle's dress and now was splitting the air with shrieks. Despite Belle's strength, she could not get up, for her body soon was pinned down even more firmly by jumping, clapping, shouting women screaming "hallelujah" and "Jesus saves."

"Lord deliver me," Belle prayed. "I'm like a fresh herring thrown to a litter of starving puppies."

In her helplessness, she realized that all those present had mistaken her fall for a "religious experience" and believed she was in ecstasy. Then and there, Belle resolved to have nothing further to do with such meetings. She had had enough. "We are not helping the Lord and we are not helping his poor," she told Miss Geer flatly. "The poor stay in their tenements, and the Lord does not come with us to such places as this." There had to be a better way to worship God in this city. And Belle determined, once more, to find it.

Then she heard of a place called Magdalene Asylum.

The big gray house on the hill was a refuge for homeless girls. It, too, held meetings at which people prayed and described their religious experiences. But Magdalene Asylum was more realistic than Miss Geer: it did not expect Jesus to solve all the problems of the poor. The men and women who worked there sheltered the homeless and fed and clothed them.

Best of all, it trained a girl to work. Work, of course, meant cooking, cleaning, washing, sewing. What other work could a woman do? An educated woman, perhaps, could be a teacher like Miss Geer. But the women who came to Magdalene Asylum, with their hunted, frightened faces and their untidy clothes, were not educated. Usually they were half-starved, demoralized young girls, picked up from around Five Points.

Soon after her disillusionment with Miss Geer's group, Belle started spending her Sundays at Magdalene Asylum where she had agreed to teach the girls domestic skills. Several times she accompanied the director of the asylum, Mr. Pierson, on recruiting trips to find more girls. The promise of a home and food and a chance to learn new skills brought girls out of Five Points who had sat, glassy-eyed and dumb, when Belle tried to attract them to one of Miss Geer's meetings.

Pierson claimed that he received his instructions for running Magdalene Asylum directly from heaven; but this did not seem strange to Belle, for she felt that she herself received messages from God. And the work that Pierson carried on, in her opinion, must certainly be pleasing to the Lord, so it was logical to suppose the Lord was willing to give Pierson the benefit of his direct guidance.

Her respect for the work of Magdalene Asylum and her respect for Pierson, added to all the painful disappointments and bright hopes accumulated over the years of her life, worked together to prepare Belle for that Sunday when Pierson was out of town and the former slave was left alone to open the door of Magdalene Asylum to a remarkable-looking stranger.

False Voices

FOURTEEN

੪ The man standing in the door of Magdalene Asylum had a silky red beard and long hair parted down the middle. His voice was thin and high.

"I have come to speak with Master Pierson."

Belle looked at him cautiously.

"Master Pierson is away," she said.

The man paused. "Just tell him that Matthias will return next Sunday," he said, and left.

Where had she seen that beard and hair before? As she went about her work, Belle could not get the man's face out of her mind. The pale eyes and the long nose. Could this be the face of the man who had directed her to Lawyer Romeyne that night on the road outside Kingston when she had feared she would never get Pete back? She had never seen that man again. It had been dark on the road and she had not seen the man very clearly. But she had always believed in her heart that it had been Jesus who had met and helped her that night.

Now it seemed to her that this was the same man who had just called at Magdalene Asylum. Of late, she had heard many people say that Jesus would return soon to save mankind. A great many religious people believed this. Perhaps that day had come and this man was Jesus.

The thought kept her awake and trembling all night. She felt as though she stood on the edge of some tremendous new experience. She could hardly wait for the man's promised return to the asylum. "When he and Master Pierson talk," she decided, "I'll just stand there and pretend I'm part of the furniture, and see what he has to say."

In this fashion, Belle managed, the following Sunday, to hear a number of remarkable statements. She heard the bearded man say that the spirit of God dwelt in him and that he had been appointed by God to establish his kingdom on earth. She noticed, too, that Pierson seemed to accept this statement with no surprise.

"Last month," Pierson in turn confided to Matthias, "as I was riding on an omnibus, God's voice sounded in my ear as clear as the blast of Gabriel's trumpet. 'Pierson, Lev Pierson,' his voice said. 'Your real name, henceforth, must not be Pierson but John the Baptist.' I looked around in surprise, but no one else seemed to have noticed anything. Yet I had heard God's voice as clearly as I do yours today."

The two men stared at each other in silence. Then Pierson motioned to Belle to bring a pan of water. While she watched, each man leaned forward in turn and solemnly washed the feet of the other. Belle had often heard how Jesus had washed the feet of his disciples at his Last Supper. Now she believed herself to be witnessing an equally holy occasion. Any lingering doubt she may have had as to the identity of the stranger vanished. Respecting Pierson as she did, it was not hard for her to believe that Matthias was Jesus, returned to earth where he was so desperately needed to help the poor and the freed slaves. With all the suffering and trouble that Belle saw around her, she was happy to think Jesus' coming would no longer be delayed.

Matthias rose to go. In his long robes, he extended his arms now as if resting them on a cross. "Ours is the mustard seed kingdom which is to spread over the earth," he cried. "Our creed is truth. But no man can find truth unless he comes clean into the church."

Matthias and Pierson lost no time setting up a cooperative community. Everyone was to work together and own everything in common. They called their community "The Kingdom," and invited Belle to become one of their faithful. She accepted.

Soon she was bending over the Kingdom's laundry in the big house they had rented in a small town just outside New York. She was cooking the Kingdom's meals, sweeping its floors, caring for its various children. It was the same work she had been doing all her life. But now Belle was not getting any pay. Moreover, as her share in helping set up the Kingdom, Belle had contributed all the money she had so carefully saved to buy a house, as well as several pieces of furniture. She would have been glad to contribute much more.

But as the months passed, she began to notice that the Kingdom was not practicing the love and truth that it preached. She was the only member who seemed to do much regular work. And every day, the quarrels among its leaders grew more bitter. Pierson now was arguing the right to be leader with Matthias. And Matthias' ideas were steadily growing more extravagant. In fact, it seemed to Belle that no one in that "cooperative" community was cooperating with anyone else. Despite her need to believe, she was beginning to see she had made another terrible mistake. Matthias was no more Jesus than John Dumont had been God. "I had better get back to work in the city," Belle thought. "I am not doing the work of the Lord here."

She had another reason for wanting to return. She had grown increasingly worried about Peter, who was no longer attending school but was working now as a coachman for a friend of Miss Geer's. Pete was an unstable boy, always in trouble. His mother doubted that she had found in the Kingdom of Matthias any good reason to further neglect her boy. She made a visit back to the city to see if a former employer, a Mrs. Whiting, could use her again.

She returned to the Kingdom the next night to remove her things but had not been in the house more than a few hours when Pierson doubled up in terrible pain and, to everyone's shock, died before morning. Matthias was away. The Kingdom had no leader. It seemed to have collapsed as swiftly as it had started.

A court trial was held to determine the facts of Pierson's death. Matthias was accused of having used Belle to poison his colleague. The trial dragged on for months, with newspapers playing it up as much as they could. But at last the judge ruled that no murder had even been committed. Pierson, he said, seemed to have died quite naturally of indigestion after eating too many half-ripe blackberries.

The story of the Kingdom, however, was too sensational to be dropped. A newspaperman, hoping to make as much money from the story as possible, produced a book in which he accused Belle of having plotted Pierson's death and even described the manner in which she committed the crime. He accused her of being a black and evil witch who had destroyed the cooperative spirit of this beautiful little community. People who had never heard of the trial, or the verdict, read the book and believed every word.

But the man did not know the woman he was writing about.

Once before, a man called Gedney had thought he could ignore Belle's rights before the law. Had that really happened only five years earlier? Belle had spoken out in meeting so many times since then, she could hardly recall the person she had been that day in Kingston in 1828. Now, as on that past occasion, she began to look for someone to help her get justice.

And again she had not long to wait. A newspaperman called Gilbert Vale came to see her. "I would like the truth from you," he said. "The story of the Kingdom and Pierson's death has not yet been told as it deserves. I would like to write about it."

She looked at him and immediately trusted him.

"I have got the truth and I know it, and I will crush them with the truth," she told him firmly.

Looking at her determined, strong-featured face, Vale thought, "She can probably do anything she sets out to do."

So Gilbert Vale wrote the first accurate account of Belle's involvement with the Kingdom. He called his book: *Fanaticism, Its Source and Influence.*

Vale's book commented on Belle's "shrewd common sense and energetic manner. . . . She apparently despises every kind of pretense and has her own opinion on everything."

He was a thorough reporter, and he knew that few people would take the word of a Negro woman against that of a white person. So he traveled up to Ulster County and around New York City, collecting written testimonials from every employer or owner Belle had ever had, including John Dumont.

In his book, he recorded in their own words what her early employers thought of Belle. They had not always treated her fairly. But when asked, all spoke of the implicit confidence she had always merited from them and of her perfect honesty. Mr. Whiting, for whom Belle had worked, off and on, and to whose employ she returned after the trial, wrote emphatically, "We did and do still believe her to be a woman of extraordinary purity."

Vale persuaded Belle to sue the newspaperman who had written the previous book about her. It was her second court case, and once again she won. The court awarded her one hundred and twenty-five dollars.

That one hundred and twenty-five dollars was all she had to show for a lifetime of work. Belle's few pieces of furniture and her savings had disappeared with the break up of the Kingdom. Matthias had vanished into the West. "Well," she thought, "I have my two hands, and I have my children, if I can ever collect them around me again."

But once again, as on that day when she had claimed her freedom from John Dumont, something had changed in the tall woman with the brooding, intense eyes. Never again would Belle believe that any human had a power greater than her own to know the truth. This new belief in herself came to Belle, with all the glory of a second Freedom Day.

Go East

FIFTEEN

ঙ Belle worked for Mrs. Whiting on Canal Street for nine more years—years in which she lost her son again.

Peter had been in trouble almost since the first day his mother had brought him to New York. He had played truant so repeatedly that he was very soon expelled from the navigation school. At that time Belle and Miss Geer decided his size might be one problem. He was only eleven but as tall as most men. Perhaps a man's job would make him live up to his height. Miss Geer knew a Mr. Jones who needed a coachman.

But a year later, the boy disappeared along with his plum-colored coachman's coat and Mr. Jones' best saddle. He reappeared soon enough, but without coat or saddle, both of which he had sold, spending the money on friends. His employer did not press charges. "The boy is young," he said. "He should never have been given such a responsible job. Belle, see if you can't keep him out of further trouble."

But Belle could not control Peter. The scars on his face remained to remind her of the beatings he had suffered during his months in Alabama. It seemed to her he had never quite belonged to her after that. There was always something restless and unhappy under Pete's bright surface. And she, with her own work and her constant search for a way to do the work of her Lord, had never found enough time for him. How was she now to control her wild young son?

"With no job and no school," she confided worriedly to Miss Geer, "Pete spends too much time around the beer halls tryin' to

Canal Street in 1836, shown here where it crosses Broadway, was the street on which Belle lived during her last nine years in New York.
COURTESY MUSEUM OF THE CITY OF NEW YORK

impress those older boys. I'm worried he's going to get himself into real trouble and no Mr. Jones to let him off this time. And all these riots in the city. I just know my boy's goin' to get hurt. I don't know what to do about my Pete."

The city these days seemed like a tinder box, waiting to go up in flames. Irish immigrants had been coming in by the thousands, competing with the ex-slaves for jobs and places to live. Poorly paid (when they could find work), crowded into filthy tenements, their children hungry, the Irish blamed their sufferings on the Negroes and on the abolitionists. Wasn't it said that the abolitionists were trying to free the southern slaves, who would only take more jobs away from white men?

During the hot summer months, the heat pressed on the nerves of the poor and sent gangs of ragged Irish youth into the streets. Sometimes men seemed to go mad in the heat, setting fire to Negro homes and churches, chasing down every dark-skinned man, woman, or child they could find, beating them with stones and clubs. Sometimes these gangs were led by well-dressed men: cotton merchants, it was rumored, trying to work up the Irish against the Negroes and the abolitionists.

And things were getting worse. Life was growing even harder for the poor. More and more men were out of work. The banging of carpenters and bricklayers had slowed almost to a halt. Mr. Whiting said speculators had bought too much land, built too many buildings. Now they were laying off their workers. Yet food prices continued to climb. Flour was so expensive that the poor could not even afford bread. Men said that there was plenty of flour but that the flour merchants were hoarding it to keep the price up.

One night a mob of poor people raided the shops of the flour merchants. That was the night the Irish were seen for the first time working shoulder to shoulder with the Negroes. The streets were left powdered with white flour, but no bodies lay there the next morning. It was a new kind of riot. And, for once, the children were fed.

The longer she stayed in New York, the more convinced Belle became that this was no town for her Pete. Frequently she even caught herself wishing, for his sake, that she had never taken that steamboat to New York. But it was too late to go back. There had to be some other solution. At last, it seemed to her the only possible answer was to send her son to sea.

In that day, more than half of all American seamen were Negroes. A seaman's life was really not much better than a slave's. White men did not want such work. Many captains were cruel, and on board ship they could treat their men as they wished. The hours were long, the food poor, the quarters cramped and filthy. But if such a life could keep Peter out of prison for a few years and give him a chance to mature into a man, Belle thought it would be better than New York. She began to try to persuade her son to sign up on a whaleboat. He stubbornly refused, and he could be quite as stubborn as she.

His pranks now were landing him in jail with increasing frequency. True, they were not serious pranks—not yet. When Belle came to court to answer for him, the judge would always release him in her care, with a small fine and a warning. But within a few weeks, Pete would be in jail again. At last, she warned him that she could not answer for him anymore; next time, he would have to face the court alone. At first, Pete would not believe her, but a month later he was once again jailed and his mother refused to come to court.

Pete, never at a loss, promptly sent for a Negro minister who was well known for helping young men of his own race—and the minister accomplished what Belle could not. In return for his help, he persuaded the boy to promise to ship out on a whaling vessel.

Belle went down to the pier to see Pete's ship sail away. Watching the white sail move out to sea, she felt one more part of her life cut away. It was August, 1839.

A year later, Belle received her first letter from Pete. Mr. Whiting read it aloud.

My dear and beloved mother,
I take this opportunity to write to you and inform you that I am well and in hopes for to find you the same. I am got on board the same unlucky ship, Zone of Nantucket. I am sorry for to say that I have been punished once severely, for shoving my head in the fire for other folks. I would like to know how my sisters are. I wish you would write me an answer as soon as possible. I am your son that is so far from your home, in the wide, briny ocean. Mother, I hope you do not forget me, your dear and only son. I hope you all will forgive me for all that I have done.
Your son, PETER VAN WAGENEN

Belle dictated a reply to Mr. Whiting and carefully mailed it. And she went on scrubbing clothes, ironing shirts, making beds, cleaning floors, marketing, and cooking meals—and attending religious meetings.

She continued also, during these years, to hear a great deal of talk about Jesus returning to earth. Some said he would arrive between March 1843, and March 1844. Others said the exact day was October 22, 1844. One man she met at meetings was always jumping to his feet crying, "Prepare! Prepare for Jesus' coming!"

The first winter of Pete's absence was bitter cold. Well-to-do people living on prosperous streets grew accustomed to the sight of ragged clothing and frightened hungry faces. Almost every day men and women knocked timidly at the Whiting door looking for work. Belle brooded at the suffering she saw and the indifference of people who were better off. Sometimes, her own indifference shocked her.

She was again saving what money she could to buy a little house for her daughters. So when Mr. Whiting handed her a half-dollar one day, saying, "Get some poor man to scrub the front steps, Belle, and give him this for his trouble," she simply pocketed the coin, and set to scrubbing the step herself. As she worked, a worn-looking man stopped in front of the Whiting house. With despair in his eyes, he stared at her busy hands. The small coin weighed down her pocket like a brick. Did he know that she was taking this work away from him? "Perhaps," she thought, "he has a family at home. Because of me, there'll be no food on their table tonight. The rich rob the poor," she murmured, "but the poor rob one another."

In the years after Peter's departure, the city seemed to grow more mean and ugly in Belle's eyes. It seemed to her she was now seeing its true face in all its raw selfishness. The city had never cared for its people. It freed its slaves, then piled them into Five Points and gave them mean work or no work at all. It lured the starving from overseas with promises of work and high wages, then shut them up in crowded rabbit hutches. It turned poor against poor.

Slavery was against the law in New York. But hadn't Pete told her of finding slave pens in the cellars of private houses near the docks? He said Africans were still brought in on ships and hidden in those pens until they could be shipped south.

New York was a cotton town. Local shipowners built family fortunes by transporting southern cotton to English mills. Local mill owners grew equally prosperous, weaving the long strong threads into cloth. Bankers loaned large sums to southern planters, and prayed the planters would have a good year and no slave trouble so they could get their money back. Antislavery laws? The city government winked. Nothing must interfere with cotton.

Five months after Pete's first letter, Belle received another: "My dear mother: I have wrote you a letter before, but have received no answer from you, and was very anxious to see you." He had not received her letter. "I hope to see you in a short time," he continued. "I have had very bad luck but are in hopes to have better in time to come. I should like if my sisters are well, and all the people around the neighborhood. I expect to be home in twenty-two months or thereabouts."

Belle dictated another letter, with Mr. Whiting's help, and mailed it. And went about her work. And kept on brooding.

She had met many decent people in the city and heard of others who fought hard to keep the law. She had heard of something called a Vigilance Committee. They said the committee was small but its members were stubborn men, constantly struggling to make the city enforce the state's laws against slavery. Any fugitive slave could go to them for help, and many needed help in these days. More and more slaves were fleeing the South. They had given up all hope of ever hearing the freedom bells ring out down there.

Late in 1841 Belle received another letter. It was the third she had received. Now Pete wrote, "This is the fifth letter that I have wrote to you and have received no answer and it makes me very uneasy. So pray write as quick as you can. We are out from home, twenty-three months, and in hopes to be back home in fifteen months. I have not much to say, but tell me if you have been up home since I left or not. I want to know what sort of a time is at home. So write as quick as you can, won't you?"

At the end, he had added, "Notice—when this you see, remember me, and place me in your mind." Then, perhaps from some magazine, he had copied this poem:

> *Get me to my home, that's in the far distant west,*
> *To the scenes of my childhood, that I like the best;*
> *There the tall cedars grow, and the bright waters flow,*
> *Where my parents will greet me, white man, let me go!*
>
> *Let me go to the spot where the cataract plays,*
> *Where oft I have sported in my boyish days;*
> *And there is my poor mother, whose heart ever flows,*
> *At the sight of her poor child, to her let me go, let me go!*

Belle never heard from her son again.

As the years passed, Belle became increasingly dissatisfied with her way of life in the city. What had she to show for all her years? Had her work ever helped her or those whom she loved? It seemed to her it had only helped whatever master she served at the time. When she had saved money, it had been taken from her. And when she thought to serve God through a master, she found each time that she was far closer to God than was the man she served.

Her past mistakes lay like patches of burned forest in her mind. But sometimes, underneath, she could feel a new growth pushing up, a growth she knew in her heart would be far more beautiful than the old. More and more she began to wonder what lay ahead for her. And more and more this woman came to believe that the Lord had been preparing her for a great mission, and soon would direct her feet into that new way.

As Belle went about Mrs. Whiting's home, cleaning and cooking, she found herself expecting some kind of special message. Occasionally, she had a feeling that the words of that message had just brushed close by, like the wings of a swallow swooping low through a barn. But the message moved too fast to come clear in her mind. She would be bending over, surrounded by clouds of laundry steam or dust kicked up by her broom, or leaning over to fluff a feather mattress, when the feeling would begin to move in her. Some plan of God's was emerging as surely as a chicken from its egg. But the chicken was not yet strong enough to peck its own way through the shell.

Then, one day, the message came. She was scrubbing the kitchen floor on hands and knees, dipping her calloused hand with the stiff brush into the wooden bucket of water, when the first part of the message flashed clear—clearer than any thought she had ever had—"I am no longer Isabelle."

She looked down at her big-knuckled fingers, parched and wrinkled with housework, and at the coarsened nails. They were certainly Isabelle's. She stared down at the gaunt, muscular body. Six feet long—every inch of it Isabelle. But the spirit inside had changed. For some time now, she realized, the spirit had not been Isabelle. And with this new awareness came another: it was time she stopped being a servant to white folk. From now on she would do only the work of the Lord. What work would that be? She did not know exactly. She only knew she must leave this house and go forth, speaking the truth to the people. God had shown her his truth so that she could help other men to know it.

Belle did not waste any more time. She told no one her plans, not even her daughters up in Ulster County. She was afraid there would be too much fuss and interference.

Late one afternoon, the tall Negro woman dropped a change of clothing, a loaf of bread, some cheese, and one twenty-five-cent coin into a pillowcase. Then she knelt to pray. "Lord, I will give back all that ever I have taken away. What more wilt thou have me do?"

And it seemed to her that he answered, "Go out of the city."

And she replied, "I will go—just go."

Then it was night. And she asked, "Lord, whither shall I go?"

And the voice came, "As plain," she insisted later, "as my own voice speaking to you." And the voice said, "Go East." And that, too, seemed as it should be. Had not the wise men traveled East to find Jesus?

Then it was almost dawn, almost morning. She picked up the pillow case and walked down the three steep flights of steps from her room. Mrs. Whiting was already in the kitchen.

"The Lord's goin' to give me a new home, Mrs. Whiting, and I'm goin' away."

Mrs. Whiting looked up in amazement. "But where are you going?"

"I'm goin' East."

"What does that mean?"

"The Lord has directed me to go East and leave this city at once."

Mrs. Whiting gasped. "Belle, you've gone crazy."

"No, I ain't. I'm goin' to have a new name too."

Mr. Whiting was in the kitchen door now, straightening his collar. His wife looked at him helplessly. She was plainly worried. "Belle's crazy," she said flatly.

He looked at his wife reprovingly, "Oh, I guess not," he said, and sat calmly down to breakfast.

Mrs. Whiting was exasperated. "But I tell you she is. She says she's going out of the city, that the Lord has told her to go, and that he has told her she is going to have a new name too. Now, doesn't all that look crazy?"

"Why, no," said Mr. Whiting, smiling. Still, he urged Belle to wait a while and have a bite to eat.

It was too late for that. The spirit that was no longer Isabelle would not let this tall woman wait. Her soul was singing. Her feet were dancing for the road. She stepped through a white "master's" door for the last time and strode firmly off down Canal Street, headed east toward Brooklyn. As she walked, her pillowcase dangling from one hand, she heard for the last time the great boom of the gun from Governor's Island. That day it seemed to be saluting not the dawn over the city, but the dawn of her own new life.

Truth Shall Be My Abiding Name

S I X T E E N

¶ The woman who had been Isabelle left the city on the morning of June 1, 1843. She was at that time about forty-six years
old.

It was only a short walk from Mrs. Whiting's house to the
steam-operated ferry at the foot of Catherine Street. The ships on
the East River rocked gently in the dawn light, their tall masts
screening Brooklyn from her view. She dug deep into the pillow
case for her twenty-five-cent piece to pay the ferry. Safe on the
Brooklyn side, her feet pointed east again, and soon took her to a
sandy road leading past comfortable, neat farms.

It seemed that she walked for hours, never daring to look back. She was haunted by her memory of a tale from the Bible in which a woman very like herself had been ordered by the Lord to leave a great and evil city. This other woman, who was Lot's wife, had been forbidden by the Lord to look back on the city she was leaving. But she had not been able to resist taking one last peek, and the Lord, in punishment, had turned her into a pillar of salt.

Belle had not received any similar command from the Lord, but she preferred not to risk disaster. It was many miles before she dared turn her eyes back. By then only a low cloud of blue smoke could be seen hovering like a swarm of bees over the spot where she had last seen the great city.

Firmly she plodded on, past fields of corn and potatoes and tidy homes. She expected at any moment to receive her new name

The Fulton Ferry, as it docked in Brooklyn in 1840.
COURTESY MUSEUM OF THE CITY OF NEW YORK

from the Lord. The old name, given in slavery, would not do for God's pilgrim. And then, just as she had known it would, the new name came—quietly, like an old friend. She recognized it immediately as her name: Sojourner.

She was feeling relieved, in fact quite light-headed at this marvelous happening, when she suddenly realized that part of the lightheadedness might be the result of having refused Mr. Whiting's offer of breakfast. It was many hours since she had eaten. Surely the people at the next farm would not mind giving her a cup of water to wash down the bread and cheese she carried.

A Quaker woman in a plain gray gown cheerfully filled a cup for Belle from her well. "What is thy name?" she asked.

"Sojourner," she said.

An amused smile greeted her. *"What* is thy name?" the woman asked again.

"Sojourner."

"Where does thee get such a name as that?" asked the woman.

"The Lord has given it to me."

Now the Quaker woman was smiling broadly. "Thee gave it to thyself, did thee not? Has it been thy name long?"

"No," said Belle, quite offended.

The woman was persistent. "What was thy name before?"

"Belle."

"Belle what?"

"Belle whatever my master's name was."

"Well, thee says now thy name is Sojourner."

"Yes."

"Sojourner what?"

As Sojourner told it later, "Well, I had to confess I hadn't thought of that. And thereupon she picked my new name to pieces, and made it look so peculiar that I said to myself, 'It don't appear to be such a good name after all!' And I said, 'I must go.'

And I plodded on over the sandy road and was very hot and miserable. And in my wretchedness I said, 'Oh, God, give me a name with a handle to it. Oh, that I had a name with a handle!' And it came to me, and that same moment, like a voice as true as God is true: 'Sojourner TRUTH.' And my heart leaped for joy— Sojourner Truth. 'Why,' said I, 'thank you, God. That is a good name. Thou art my last master and thy name is Truth, so shall Truth be my abiding name until I die.'"

And so she who had taken the name Sojourner Truth walked along, following the road east, always east, across Long Island.

After many long hours, the sun at last dipped low behind her. And she began to wonder where she could find a bed. There were many prosperous-looking farms along the way. She spotted one in particular that appeared so large she felt it must have innumerable corners in which a stranger could curl up and remain safely out of the way until morning.

But the man who answered her knock barely opened the door before shutting it again. "No room," he grunted.

The second house was almost as large, but the woman in the door said, rather embarrassed, that she was "expecting company." In this way, Sojourner must have knocked on as many as twenty doors. Not one had room for a stranger. But she had begun to notice that the smaller the house, the friendlier the face that appeared in the door.

Her legs ached. She had had no supper. It was dark and lonely on the sandy road. A few stars and the slender curve of a new moon were all that remained to light her way. Suddenly, she almost stumbled into the arms of two men who looked to her like Indians. "How far to the next tavern?" she asked quickly. She had no money but perhaps she could work for her bed.

The taller man eyed her curiously from between two thick plaits of hair. "About two miles," he said. "Are you alone?"

She did not care to satisfy his curiosity and decided God's company was reason enough for her to answer, "Not exactly."

She walked hastily on.

Soon she came to a building. It seemed larger than taverns she had known and the moon plainly glinted on iron bars in several of its windows. She followed a light to an open door and found inside a heavy-set man straightening out tables and chairs near a long wooden bar. "Just this room here's the tavern," he explained. "But it ain't got no bed. The rest of the building is courthouse and jail. 'Course I could let you stay the night in jail. But I'd have to lock you in."

She was not ready to agree to that suggestion. Perhaps he would not let her out again. Sojourner preferred to walk on alone under the stars.

A little farther along the road, Sojourner spotted a tiny shed— no bigger than a manger to shelter a single donkey but, she thought, big enough for a tired woman to lie down. She bent over, only to find a white couple already sleeping on the straw. "Do you know where I may get a room for the night?" she inquired politely.

Both sleepers sat up in a panic. Then, seeing only the tall form in its neat, sober dress, they smiled. "Why come right in with us," said the woman. And she and her husband moved over, insisting Sojourner take the better half of their straw.

As Sojourner Truth lay in the dark of that tiny shed, she could not help but remark to herself that these people seemed to feel no lack of room. And yet they had less of it than any person she had asked for lodging that entire night.

A few more such experiences and Sojourner was convinced that the rich understood the rich and the poor the poor, and what a man could be persuaded to give another man had little enough to do with what he had to give.

She said afterward, "I never could find out that the rich had any religion. But if I had been rich and accomplished, I could have. For the rich could always find religion in the rich, and I could always find it among the poor."

Not many days later, Sojourner came upon a huge, outdoor religious meeting. She had never attended a camp meeting. Thousands of families were camped around the field, living in wagons, crude tents, and huts hastily thrown together from loose branches. The food Sojourner saw around her would have fed the entire population of Five Points for a week. The people spent their time standing around or sitting on provision boxes, listening to anyone who cared to speak. The meeting had just started and was to last three days. Before it was over, Sojourner was granted permission to speak and to tell her story.

She described to the crowd the day she had started to return to Dumont, and instead had found Jesus. The people around her became absorbed in her story as she told them of the sufferings of slaves in Ulster County, and the sins she had watched men commit against each other in the great city she had so recently left. She talked a long time, and then, in her deep strange voice that seemed to turn every song she sang into something of her own, she sang:

> *We are going home; we soon shall be*
> *Where the sky is clear, and the soil is free;*
> *Where the victors' song floats over the plains,*
> *And the seraphs' anthem blends with the strains.*

After the meeting she stayed a long time to exchange religious ideas, and found many people who were interested in discussing them with her.

As Sojourner trudged on over the island, in the weeks that followed, she stumbled on more such meetings. Whenever possible, she asked to address them and stayed late to argue her ideas about Jesus and God. And she never failed to include a song or two. Few people at these meetings had ever heard such singing or listened to a Negro speak up in public. Men talked about Sojourner Truth, and as the tall, dark woman with the searching eyes, the powerful voice, and the original turn of speech walked through town after town, she found she was building a reputation. She could even call her own meetings now and collect a good audience.

Although she had never learned to read, her memory was extraordinary. She remembered almost everything she heard and could quote more Scriptures than many a man who could read. But she liked to put things in her own words. She determined now to know the entire Bible by heart—to understand for herself the questions raised in its pages, so that she could form her own interpretation of the thinking of Jesus.

When she had needed someone to read to her in the past, she had always asked an adult. But Sojourner found it difficult, if not impossible, to get an adult to read a passage aloud for a second time, exactly as it was written. The adult always wanted to explain the passage, as if Sojourner's difficulty lay in understanding the meaning of the words. She wanted to find her own way back to Jesus' original teaching. When she asked to hear a passage twice she did not want the person reading to scramble the thought behind the passage even more by adding his thoughts too.

So she began to ask little children, instead of adults, to read to her. The smaller her reader, the prouder he or she was to read aloud to this great, tall woman. They were so patient in repeating a passage, so pleased to be able to do it word for word, just as it lay on the page. Sojourner Truth became a familiar sight at camp meetings, seated in a circle of children, each waiting for a turn to read.

She proceeded on foot across Long Island, a dignified wanderer in her neat gown and bright bandanna, striding along the sandy roads. Wherever people would listen, she spoke. Where they would take her in, she slept. Where they needed help, she stopped to work. But she would never accept much pay for the work, saying, "God will provide."

Thus, in her solitary pilgrimage, the woman who had been Isabelle reached the town of Huntington, Long Island, and there took a boat across Long Island Sound to Connecticut.

Wild Young Men

SEVENTEEN

&❧ Once in Connecticut, Sojourner looked around for an amanuensis, a public secretary, so she could dictate a letter to her
daughters. She knew they must be worried, as they had had no
word from their mother since her sudden departure from the city.

After mailing her letter to Ulster County, she set forth again,
trudging over country roads, through town after town. She was
headed northeast now, "lecturin' some, and workin' some along
the way to get wherewith to pay tribute to Caesar."

Near Hartford, she was surprised to find many people standing
idly around in the streets and fields. When she inquired, she

learned that they were awaiting the second coming of Jesus. Their crops stood unharvested. Village stores were closed. Many had quit jobs they had held for years in order to be ready to follow Jesus as soon as he might appear. Others expected the end of the world to coincide with his arrival, and just lay quietly on their beds awaiting that day.

It all seemed pretty silly to Sojourner Truth. But no matter how strange a person's opinions might appear to her, she always enjoyed listening to them and arguing her own point of view. Moreover, she enjoyed the respectful attention she herself could arouse when voicing her own opinions.

Everywhere she passed, people seemed to be seeking new answers, new excitements. Those who listened to Sojourner at religious meetings were not interested in abolition or the sufferings of slaves as such; they were interested in hearing new religious ideas. Sojourner Truth's ideas, springing from the experiences of a life so unlike their own, appeared strange, and yet they made good

An artist's interpretation of the fervor and excitement that enraptured audiences at many camp meetings. Copyright 1838.
COURTESY NEW YORK HISTORICAL SOCIETY

sense. Her unusual way of making her point, her witty, no-nonsense approach to complicated questions, delighted her listeners. And her singing overwhelmed them.

People told their friends about this amazing six-foot, ebony-skinned woman. Her audiences grew. And with her audience grew her own belief in herself and in her power to express her thoughts and to command her listeners' attention.

One night Sojourner found herself at a camp meeting in a huge open field. There was a substantial crowd, but something had gone wrong. From a distance, her ears picked up the wolf calls, hoots, yells, and whistles. As she drew closer, she realized that a gang of hoodlums scattered through the crowd was making it impossible for the meeting to start. She could hear them urging each other on.

"Mob the speakers."

"Burn the tents."

"Break down the stand."

She shivered. For a moment their cries had brought back the cries of the mobs chasing Negroes and abolitionists through the streets of New York. Sojourner Truth was the only Negro here. Would they come after her? She would not wait to find out. Wrapping her skirts tightly about her long shanks, Sojourner hastily ducked into the nearest tent and crouched behind a trunk.

That turned out to be very little protection. The tent soon was pitching and rocking around her like a fishing boat in a Hudson Valley storm, as the crowd thrust against it in panic. But worse than the danger was her shame at hiding behind that trunk. "Should a servant of God run away from the devil?" she murmured. "Is it not written, 'One shall chase a thousand, and two put ten thousand to flight?' Where is my faith? Surely there are not a thousand devils here. I'll go to the rescue. The Lord will know how to protect me."

And with that, as she recalled later, she felt such a courage within her breast. "Oh," she said, "I felt as if I had three hearts, and that they were so large my body could hardly hold them."

Raising herself to her full height, Sojourner moved determinedly out of the dark tent. Outside, she stumbled against several men, but they only gaped foolishly when she suggested they help her quiet the riot. She strode forward without them, a tall, thin, figure in long, full skirts, moving firmly across the rough ground, in and out of patches of moonlight. She was heading straight for the rabble. Beyond it, she could see the woman who was to have been the main speaker cowering on the preacher's stand.

Sojourner turned in the opposite direction and climbed to the top of a small rise. She stood there for a moment, catching her breath, her figure straight as a Catskill hemlock. Then her head went back and the full force of her voice rose above the confusion:

> *It was early in the morning,*
> *It was early in the morning,*
> *Just at the break of day, . . .*

There was a rush like a pack of starved hounds at a rabbit, and Sojourner found herself encircled by muscular youths. She stared down into open, silent mouths, at sticks and stones clutched in grimy hands. But she did not stop singing:

> *When he rose*
> *When he rose*
> *When he rose,*
> *And went to heaven on a cloud.*

The circle narrowed. Her singing stopped abruptly.

"Why do you come about me with clubs and sticks? I am not doing harm to anyone."

The mouths below her all began to move at once.

"We aren't a-going to hurt you, old woman. We come to hear you sing."

"Sing to us, old woman."

"Talk to us, old woman."

"Pray, old woman."

"Tell us your experience."

"You stand and smoke so near me, I can neither sing nor talk," she scolded.

Several clubs were immediately thrust under her nose. Sojourner caught her breath. But the clubs were only maintaining order.

"Stand back," roared several voices. The circle loosened around Sojourner. "Now keep back. We'll knock down the first man who touches the old woman."

As she looked down into the flushed, rough faces, Sojourner comforted herself that there must be some good in all of God's children. And she began to speak to them of her religious ideas. To her surprise, they listened. When she had finished they asked many questions, and she answered those as best she could. As long as they were listening, they remained quiet. But it was like crooning a teething baby to sleep. As soon as she stopped singing or talking, they would begin their restless moving about, with roars and yells for more.

Meanwhile, the circle around her grew larger. Those in back complained that they could not hear. Someone yelled, "Climb up on a wagon and talk to us from there."

Sojourner looked doubtful. "You might turn it over," she said.

"They will not," roared the crowd's leader. "Any man who

dares hurt you, we'll knock him down instantly."

And the chorus agreed. "We won't turn it over. Nobody will hurt you."

Sojourner peered across the field. The religious meeting was now in full progress. She decided to keep these young men here a little longer. She turned her eyes back to them and began. "Well, there are two congregations on this ground. It is written that there shall be a separation, and the sheep shall be separated from the goats. The other preachers have the sheep. I have the goats. And I have a few sheep among my goats, but they are very ragged." The youths roared with appreciation.

She talked until she was weary and was beginning to wonder how she could ever bring all this to an end. But each time she paused, the air filled with cries. "More, more." "Sing." "Sing more."

At last she lifted her hand for silence.

"Children," she said, hoarsely. "I have talked and sung to you, as you asked. And now I have a request. Will you grant it?"

"Yes, yes." Every voice in the pack appeared to join in that chorus.

"If I sing one more hymn for you, will you go away and leave us this night in peace?"

"Yes, yes," the voices seemed less certain. To Sojourner's ear they sounded no stronger than the faint yelping of puppies. She was not satisfied. "I want an answer from you all, now. I will sing you one more song. In return, you will go away, and leave us this night in peace."

"Yes, yes." A little stronger. She took confidence, and her voice boomed over their heads. "I repeat my request once more. And I want you all to answer. If I sing you one more hymn, will you go away and leave us this night in peace?"

"YES!" A solid roar now.

"Amen. It is sealed," she said. There was quiet, and she began:

I bless the Lord I've got my seal, today and today,
To slay Goliath in the field, today and today.
The good old way is a righteous way,
I mean to take the kingdom in the good old way.

It was one of her favorite hymns. She sang verse after verse until there were no more verses to sing. Then she stopped. Her throat ached. She closed her eyes wearily. Would the youths go away now?

She heard a swishing across the grass. It was the feet of her wild young men, sweeping in a solid pack through the field. For a moment, heart in mouth, she feared they were rushing the speaker's stand. The audience was already falling back in panic. But no. Without so much as a glance at the stand or a break in stride, Sojourner's audience was past the stand and off the grounds.

She tramped on. Through Connecticut and into Massachusetts, a strange yet increasingly familiar figure, lecturing and working, working and lecturing. And always singing.

It happened ever more frequently now that she would find a friend behind a door on which she knocked for shelter. But not frequently enough. Sometimes, when night fell, she still had difficulty finding lodging.

The road Sojourner Truth had taken that morning in New York was indeed beginning to seem long. She had traveled it for many weeks now—walking, talking, and singing all the way. She was tired, and she found herself beginning to long for some quiet place where she might rest for a while.

Friends she met in Springfield, Massachusetts, thought they knew just the place for her. It was a new community where educated people lived in a plain and simple manner, working together to build a world of love and fellowship. These people were abolitionists and would welcome an ex-slave to join in their work. Sojourner would surely be welcome there.

Brotherhood

EIGHTEEN

꿍 And so that winter Sojourner Truth joined the Northampton Association of Education and Industry, located in Florence, Massachusetts, just outside the town of Northampton. The day she arrived, the wind whined across a monotonous stretch of snow-covered meadow. On the meadow's edge, she could see a square building squatting by the ice-locked river. On one side of the building, rows of tall, thin trees shivered in the freezing wind. On the other, a few naked willows cast forlorn shadows against grim brick walls.

Sojourner found herself shivering too. The place looked as dreary as the Ulster County prison.

She had been warned that the community was young. The Northampton Association had bought this factory building, only two years earlier, to house its members and its silk-weaving machinery. Raising silkworms and making silk cloth was the community's way of earning a living. It was a cooperative community, which meant all things were owned in common—just as they had been in the Kingdom of Matthias.

When she walked into the building, Sojourner was even more disappointed than she had been with its outside. The machinery had been given the best room, while sixty-five people took what was left. Men, women, and families were cramped into tiny apartments and bunk rooms, with only thin unpainted boards separating the rooms.

In the first moment that she stood there Sojourner heard the whir and shriek of machinery, a baby squawling, children quarreling, a woman complaining to her husband, a rock hitting an upstairs floor (perhaps it was only a shoe falling). Already her sharp eye had spotted more than one missing button or torn pair of pants on the untidy children running around. The educated ladies seemed to have no idea how to keep house. Stooped over the silk-weaving machinery, they neglected everything else in their efforts to learn to run it properly. The pins were falling from their long hair and their clothing was untidy.

Were these the educated and refined people Sojourner had been promised? Where was the community of beauty and elegance they were supposed to be creating? Everything seemed cold, comfortless, untidy. It was hardly a quiet resting place. But having come this far she did not want to appear rude. The man showing her around had introduced himself as George Benson. He had been very kind. She accepted his invitation to dinner and to spend the night.

Supper was served in the factory dining room. The codfish was too salty and the soggy potatoes looked almost as gray as the ones for which she had been reprimanded many years ago by John Dumont. But she heard no complaints from the other diners.

Benson introduced her to the cooks, a slender dignified woman and her two handsome daughters. Benson explained that, like most other workers here, these women had taken up their work at the Association without previous experience. The woman's husband was a professor of oriental languages at Harvard. At one time, the entire family had lived in India with eighteen servants to do their work. Now this woman chose to cook for the Northampton Association.

Strangely, as she listened, the food began to taste better to Sojourner Truth. She was beginning to notice in it, she thought, a certain delicious seasoning of brotherhood.

Which of these people were the true leaders of the community, she wondered? No one received any special deference, except perhaps the old blind man seated at the far end of the table. The children, in particular, would not let him alone. They showed him to his place, made sure his plate was heaped full, ran to get him what he needed, pushed each other aside to stand closest to him. The blind man was the only other Negro at the table.

There was a great deal of talk about silk-weaving machinery. The machinery had broken down—not for the first time, she gathered. Nobody seemed to know anything about repairing it, but everybody felt responsible for trying.

That night, Sojourner Truth heard many strange names. But the name of Jesus was not once mentioned. In fact, harsh things were said about the churches. She heard one man insist they were bulwarks of American slavery. "The only rights they worry about are the rights of the slaveowners," he said. Others nodded.

Benson smiled at her expression. He explained that the Association had no formal religion. Some members were Quakers. Some called themselves vegetarians. Some just followed their conscience, professing not even to believe in God. But they all had two beliefs in common: they were firmly antislavery and believed with equal firmness in the equality of men. Indeed, she could plainly see that people here not only preached but practiced equality. "No one hands down the law here," said Benson. "Every one of us has an equal voice in decisions. Except the children. I am afraid we do deny them the vote."

Voting? Sojourner had never done that. As a Negro in New York, she would have had to own property to vote, although white people could vote without it. She thought now that it would be good to vote.

Benson was asking her, "You will stay until Sunday, won't you? William Lloyd Garrison will be addressing our Sunday meeting. I know you will find him interesting. You, too, can say whatever you please at the meeting. Anyone can speak up, whether man or woman." He grinned slyly. "You don't have to be afraid. We'll treat you well. But we may not agree with your point of view and we may ask difficult questions."

Sojourner's eyes sparkled. She loved to debate. She knew from experience that few could best her. She had her own twists and turns and quick retorts from the Bible to use against her opponents. She could hardly wait for the meeting.

As she looked around and listened to the talk, the untidy hair of the ladies, the sloppy dress of the children, and the poor food, all began to seem very unimportant. There was no pretense here, no laziness. These people were doing God's work—helping bring the Brotherhood of Man a little closer to this world. Perhaps she, too, could put her shoulder to that wheel. Looking around her at the soiled clothing on the children, she thought, "They could use a good laundress."

And so Sojourner Truth became chief laundress for the Northampton Association. The records show she was one of the most useful members of the community and much respected. Like everyone else, she worked ten hours a day.

"We reduced it from eleven hours only a few weeks ago," said Benson. "After voting on the question, of course. Some of our members felt it was wrong to reduce our work day before American workers won their fight for the ten-hour day. But others felt we should set an example."

In any case it was a far shorter working day than Sojourner was accustomed to. In addition, she had so many helpers. On Mondays the head silk dyer always came down to help her wring out the clothes. He had time to spare because his department was slow at the start of the week. And there were always children around, begging to be useful.

Then spring came, bringing a hundred surprises. The flat meadow was dotted with wild flowers. Mulberry leaves budded on the thin trees she had noticed from the road that first day. Their leaves provided food for the silk worms. The ice melted and revealed below its broken surface the water of the Mill River flowing in a dark stream from the distant wooded hills. Straggling tendrils of arbutus trailed pink blossoms, and laurel bloomed just as it did every year in Ulster County. How could she ever have believed this to be a desolate spot?

Sojourner had not been many months at Northampton before she had met most of the antislavery men whose names she had heard at table her first night. William Lloyd Garrison had walked in that first Sunday, a tall man with a long gaunt face and eyes that seemed mild behind their thick spectacles. "Prejudice against color is rebellion against God," he had repeated several times. Garrison passionately hated slavery. He would do anything; if need be, he would urge dissolution of the union itself to get rid of it. His weekly newspaper *The Liberator* was read aloud at the

Northampton Association. "No union with slaveholders," shouted its masthead.

One night Garrison burst in out of a storm, accompanied by a heavy-set young man. "Frederick Douglass will be speaking in Northampton tomorrow. I have invited him to stay the night," he said.

The younger man had a massive head with a thick mane of springy black hair arching over a wide, bronze forehead. Sojourner particularly noticed the piercing, intent eyes of this fugitive slave from Maryland. She knew he had been working with the antislavery men only a short time, but already he was considered one of the most powerful of their speakers. She had heard Garrison's description of his first meeting with Douglass on Nantucket Island, where both men had been asked to speak. "I think I never hated slavery so intensely," Garrison had said. "When he had finished speaking, I climbed to the platform and I called out to our audience: 'Have we been listening to a thing, a piece of property, or to a man?' And five hundred voices shouted back at me, 'A man, a man.' And when I asked them, 'Will you protect him as a brother man?' they roared back at me 'Yes,' with such vehemence I thought the walls and roof of the meeting hall would tumble in."

Sojourner noticed Douglass put his arm around the shoulders of the old blind Negro, David Ruggles. Ruggles had been an editor and doctor in New York for many years and secretary of the underground New York Vigilance Committee, which helped fugitive slaves passing through New York. He was a freeborn man but had never thought himself above helping those of his race who were less fortunate. One of the slaves he had helped was Frederick Douglass.

"It was the strain of my work for the Vigilance Committee that blinded me," Ruggles had explained to Sojourner. "After I lost my sight, I had no way to earn a living. I was almost reduced to living in the street when George Benson heard of my trouble and came down to find me and bring me up here to Northampton. He came just in time. I don't know what I would have done if I had had to live another month like that."

The children at Northampton loved the blind man with the sensitive doctor's fingers and the wonderful stories. He would tell them of rescuing runaway slaves from the very grasp of the slave catchers, shifty-eyed little men who lurked in muddy alleys or around salty docks, ready for a price to send other men back into slavery. Or he would tell of street fights and ships riding at anchor in the dark, and sailors who could be trusted, and sometimes he would even tell of a friendly captain who knew when to look the other way while a fugitive was lowered over the side. And then there were the court battles to describe.

Wherever Ruggles went children popped up like rabbits in his path. George Benson's nephew, Matthew, who had the special honor of leading the blind doctor to his bath, had fought hard for that right. But there were always flocks of other children around, asking Ruggles to "feel whose muscle is coming on best," and the old man never failed carefully and solemnly to press each small arm with his experienced fingers before offering a final professional judgment.

Sojourner's special friend at Northampton was Sam Hill. Like Benson he was a founder of the cooperative colony. He had once been a member of a Baptist church, but that association ended when he sponsored an antislavery meeting that the abolitionist leader Wendell Phillips was supposed to address. Hill recognized the leader of the mob that broke up his meeting, that night, as a deacon from his own church, and promptly withdrew his membership from that church.

Sojourner came to know Phillips, too, at Northampton. The

Boston aristocrat was one of the most effective abolitionist speakers. People called him "abolition's golden trumpet." Sojourner found him to be a man of rare sweetnesss, but a man also of firm principle. Frederick Douglass liked to tell how Phillips once had walked a steamboat deck with him all night long, rather than take a berth with the other white passengers when the captain would not provide one for Douglass.

Parker Pillsbury was another famous abolitionist who regularly visited the Northampton Association. Big, rough-voiced, with a great black beard, he looked every inch the village blacksmith his father had been, and he was as stubborn as he looked. Pillsbury had been a Congregational minister. But his pulpit had cramped his soul. He wanted to rouse people to fight slavery, and he found that easier to do outside the church. Nevertheless, he traveled around New England with other abolitionist speakers, attending services wherever possible. He or his friends would rise up unexpectedly in the congregation and demand that the minister say a few words against slavery. Such interruptions were rarely welcomed. Once a mob chased Pillsbury and tore his long frock coat from collar to skirt. He continued to wear the coat for years and would wheel proudly on the speaker's platform to show off the great rent down the back.

These men that Sojourner met at Northampton attacked the churches, the government, the constitution, the judges, the merchants, the bankers. They seemed afraid of nobody and nothing. They blew like great storms, blasting every institution and every individual who dared defend the right of one man to own another. "I will be as harsh as truth," Garrison had said, "and as uncompromising as justice."

Many years later, remembering those years at Northampton, Sojourner sighed, "What good times we had. If any were infidels,

I wish the world were full of such infidels. Religion without humanity is poor human stuff."

Her life at the Association lasted three years. Then her quiet resting place vanished. The silk business was in trouble, and the community could not pay its debts. George Benson bought the factory building, Sam Hill the silk. For Sojourner Truth, one more earthly "Kingdom" had collapsed. Once again she had no money, no home, and worst of all, no work at hand that she could believe was useful in the eyes of her Lord.

She was cooking and cleaning house for a living again, at first working for George Benson, then for other citizens around Northampton. One day her good friend, Sam Hill, came to her. He insisted on building her a house of her own, so that she would still have a resting place to come back to, even though the Association was gone. He said she could pay him the three hundred dollars when she was able. Her "X" on his mortgage, he said, was better in his eyes than the flowing signature of Boston's biggest banker.

Well, she had waited since Freedom Day to own her own home, always dreaming of the day she would gather her children together. More than twenty years had passed since that dream had first taken shape in her mind. Now her daughters were all grown. Diana still worked for Dumont; the others had married and moved away from New Paltz. But even with a house of her own, Sojourner Truth herself was in no mood to settle down. She had sensed a new mission in the struggle against slavery. She did not yet know what her particular task in the abolition struggle should be, but she was convinced the Lord once again would point out her way.

About this time a friend from the Northampton Association, Olive Gilbert, suggested that she help Sojourner put down her life story. Frederick Douglass and a number of other fugitive slaves recently had published their autobiographies. Their books were proving powerful weapons in the antislavery struggle. But so far all the books published had been about men, and all of them about slavery in the South. What about a woman, a slave in New York? Sojourner could prove slavery was not just bad in the South, but terrible anywhere.

But Olive Gilbert pointed out that Sojourner might have a great deal of trouble finding a publisher. She was not a famous abolitionist speaker like Douglass and she was a woman, and black. Never mind. She could pay for the printing herself from the sales of her book. Of course few bookstores would be interested in selling it. Well, Sojourner Truth would just have to peddle the book herself.

The two women approached Garrison with their idea.

"Wonderful," he said. "A book by Sojourner Truth would be a great contribution to our cause. I can quite probably get Mr. Yerrington who prints *The Liberator* to do Sojourner's book on credit. And don't worry about any difficulty selling it. I'll recommend the book myself at every meeting I address. Just be present when I do, Sojourner. You'll sell your entire first edition in no time."

Garrison wrote an introduction: ". . . It is hoped that the perusal of the following narrative may increase the sympathy that is felt for the suffering colored population of this country, and inspire to renewed efforts for the liberation of all who are pining in bondage on American soil. . . ."

Sojourner's book appeared as a thin brown paper-covered volume with her picture for a frontispiece. The picture had been made many years earlier, perhaps around the time the Kingdom of Matthias fell apart. It is the oldest picture we have of Sojourner Truth. It shows a woman of great dignity and calm, with a determined face, strong-featured and composed, and eyes that look directly at the camera. Under the edge of the white bandanna on her head, the hair looks black. A dark alpaca gown falls in broad pleats across her bosom and a white neckerchief is tucked carefully around her neck.

Actually, by the time her book appeared, Sojourner's hair was graying, and she wore the gold-rimmed spectacles given to her at the Northampton Association to help her with the ironing. She was older than the picture in her book, but otherwise not very different. Olive Gilbert called Sojourner's book, *Narrative of*

The title page and frontispiece of the first edition of the Narrative of Sojourner Truth, *1850. The date (1828) given for her emancipation was an error on the part of Olive Gilbert. The correct date was July 4, 1827.*
COURTESY SCHOMBURG COLLECTION, NEW YORK PUBLIC LIBRARY

SOJOURNER TRUTH.

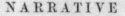

NARRATIVE

OF

SOJOURNER TRUTH

A

NORTHERN SLAVE,

EMANCIPATED FROM BODILY SERVITUDE BY THE STATE

NEW YORK, IN 1828.

WITH A PORTRAIT.

'Sweet is the virgin honey, though the wild bee store it in a reed;
And bright the jewelled band that circleth an Ethiop's arm;
Pure are the grains of gold in the turbid stream of the Ganges;
And fair the living flowers that spring from the dull cold sod.
Wherefore, thou gentle student, bend thine ear to my speech,
For I also am as thou art; our hearts can commune together:
To meanest matters will I stoop, for mean is the lot of mortal;
I will rise to noblest themes, for the soul hath a heritage of glory.'

BOSTON:

PRINTED FOR THE AUTHOR.

Sojourner Truth: A Northern Slave. It first appeared in 1850.

Once more, Sojourner Truth stepped out onto the New England dirt roads, in her long, full skirt and heavy walking shoes. She had been a slave. And she had been freed, in part through her own efforts. Now she would help free others. The Lord had pointed out her new task. It would be to testify against slavery.

Testifyin'

NINETEEN

&❧ It was in the year 1850 that Sojourner Truth first set out to
testify against slavery and to sell her _Narrative_. It proved a good
year to sell such a book. Congress had just passed the Fugitive
Slave Bill, and the disputes surrounding it had aroused more than
the usual interest in slavery. Although the bill was now law, the
abolitionists felt it had to be opposed. Sojourner's book could
help.

Before the Fugitive Slave Bill, a runaway slave who had
crossed into a free state generally had been safe from legal recapture. But the new bill forced the marshals of free states to hunt

down fugitives within their borders and return them to their masters. Even a free Negro was not safe; it took only the word of two white men to prove a Negro a fugitive. The accused had no jury at his trial and was not even allowed to testify in his own defense. Moreover, the fee of the commissioner who ruled on a fugitive case was doubled if he ruled in the slaveowner's favor. Even sympathetic people now hesitated to help a runaway and risk having to pay an enormous fine.

The abolitionists said the new law was a mockery of justice. "It only proves the desperation of the slaveowners," they said. "Thousands of the South's best workers are fleeing North every year. The new bill is supposed to discourage slaves from running away by making it more difficult for them to escape."

The abolitionists also pointed out that while it was true the South had great power in Congress, the bill would never have passed without the support of northern politicians. Had not even the Senator from Massachusetts, Daniel Webster, himself, voted in its favor?

Garrison and his friends were angry, but they were jubilant, too; they knew the bill would be impossible to enforce. Right now the northern man-in-the-street cared nothing about slavery, one way or the other. But wait until he saw the South trying to tell him how to treat people in his own backyard. The bill would only breed more abolitionists.

The Garrisonians began calling meetings. They demanded more speakers, looked for more fugitives who could tell their simple yet terrible stories from public platforms. In Boston, leading citizens hastily formed "committees of vigilance and alarm" to protect any Negro who might need it. Sojourner Truth began to appear regularly at abolitionist meetings near Boston—and to peddle her book.

For a while her book was her voice. She would appear in the crowd, moving austerely among the people, an extraordinary-looking woman with her great height and air of authority, quietly selling a book. True to his promise, Garrison always announced her presence. But one day he went further and asked her to join him on the platform. "Sojourner Truth will say a few words," he said. "And Wendell Phillips will follow."

Sojourner remembered later that she had shivered at the thought of preceding a spellbinder such as Wendell Phillips. She was certain the crowd would forget her while listening to him, and certainly would forget that she had a book to sell. "What can I do," she wondered, "to make them remember me?" It would have to be something Wendell Phillips could not do.

She decided to sing them a song she had made up herself. A "homemade song" as she called it. She had never sung for an abolitionist crowd, but she had thrilled many camp meetings with her hymns. She was sure these people would listen as closely.

Her song had many verses. She sang them all in her sonorous, deep voice.

I am pleading for my people,
A poor downtrodden race,
Who dwell in freedom's boasted land,
With no abiding place.

I am pleading that my people
May have their rights restored;
For they have long been toiling,
And yet have no reward.

They are forced the crops to culture,
But not for them they yield,
Although both late and early
They labor in the field.

Whilst I bear upon my body
The scars of many a gash,
I am pleading for my people
Who groan beneath the lash.

Later, when Phillips was speaking, Sojourner noticed almost every paragraph of his speech seemed to start with her name. "As my friend, Sojourner Truth, puts it so well . . . ," he would say, and then continue with his own observations. She thought, "Even if they had wanted to, he would never have let them forget me."

After the meeting, people rushed over to buy her book. They wanted to buy her song, too. She was surprised; she had never thought of having her songs printed. But after this experience, Sojourner always brought along songs to sell. She sold them for five or ten cents. Occasionally, someone would ask, "What tune goes with this song?" Sojourner would shrug her shoulders. If a person had a mind to sing, she felt, he should be able to find his own tune.

About this time, she also began to sell copies of her photograph. She called it her "shadow," and across the bottom of each she had printed, "I sell the shadow to support the substance."

Songs and photographs helped pay her way. But the money she received for her book was carefully put aside to pay the printer and the mortgage on the house Sam Hill had built for her.

That summer, Sojourner accepted an invitation to serve as a delegate from Massachusetts to the first national Woman's Rights Convention, which was to be held in Worcester. The idea of such a meeting was a bold, new one. Most people thought it downright impudent. As Sojourner walked along the Worcester streets she could not help but overhear the remarks.

"Do these ladies want to put on men's pants too?" asked one man.

"Outrageous," sniffed a woman.

"Did you hear what our minister said yesterday?" A fat man was speaking. "He really put it square. He said, 'This evening at town hall, a hen will attempt to crow.'"

The group burst into laughter, then stopped abruptly to stare after Sojourner.

Newspapers called it the Hen Convention, and one minister threatened to expel from his church any member who dared even attend the meeting. The women participating were jeered and hooted at as they passed through the streets.

Looking around the convention hall that first day, Sojourner

An early caricature showing the popular prejudice against the Woman's Rights Movement.

COURTESY NEW YORK HISTORICAL SOCIETY

TWO OF THE FE'HE MALES.

noticed that the newspapers had overlooked a good many roosters in naming the convention for its hens. She noticed Frederick Douglass, Garrison, Pillsbury, Phillips, and many other abolitionist friends. Sojourner was the only Negro woman there, the only woman who knew what it was to be a servant and a slave. All the others were educated white women. Some of the questions they argued were strange to Sojourner. One delegate asked indignantly, "Should a woman not have the legal right at least to retain her own silver and jewelry if she divorces her husband?"

Sojourner reacted impatiently to such a question. There were more important things to solve. Once, when asked her opinion, she replied, "Sisters, I'm not clear what you be after. If women want any rights more than they've got, why don't they just take them and not be talking about it."

But as the convention progressed, she grew more appreciative of many of her companions there, even though their backgrounds did differ so much from her own. She nodded understandingly when tiny, gentle Lucretia Mott spoke of how as a teacher she was paid only half what male teachers were getting. Nor did it seem strange to hear good-natured Lucy Stone explain that she would keep her own name and refuse to use her husband's name when she married in order to show the world that her husband was not her master.

The chairman had opened the meeting by warning the delegates, "Our claim must rest on its justice and conquer by its power of truth. . . . We claim for women all the blessings which the other sex has, solely, or by her aid, achieved for itself."

These, too, were words that a woman who had been a slave could fully accept. Moreover Sojourner found many women at this convention who fought as hard for abolition as they did for women's rights. "Open a man's eyes to one kind of injustice," they argued, "and it will be easier to open his eyes to another."

At its close, the convention adopted as its motto, "Equality before the law without distinction of sex or color." All present pledged to fight for woman's right to vote and the repeal of all property laws discriminating against her.

As the last session was breaking up, one member read Sojourner the comments of a New York newspaper, "Woman's offices are those of wife, mother, daughter, sister, friend—Good God, can they not be content with these?" When in her life, Sojourner wondered, had she ever been given a chance to really carry out any of the roles that this paper insisted belonged to her as a woman?

At the convention, she had been greatly amused at the costume adopted by some of the women. They wore what they called "bloomers," claiming these freed the body so the limbs could develop better and women could be more active. The garment reminded Sojourner of the slave cloth she had sewn up between her legs many years ago, when the strip given her for a dress had proved too short for a six-foot girl. Bloomers might seem a symbol of freedom to some women, but a long, full skirt was the symbol of emancipation to Sojourner Truth.

Although Sojourner sold many copies of her *Narrative* during the three days of the Worcester meeting, she continued to worry about the great debt she owed Mr. Yerrington, the printer. Many more copies must be sold, she knew, before she could pay off this debt. She confided her worry to Garrison before he left the convention. He replied, "I will be leaving on a lecture tour with George Thompson, the English abolitionist, in several months. Why not come with us? You'll have many good chances along the way to sell your book."

Sojourner hesitated. "I have no money for such a long trip."

"Never mind," he said. "I'll gladly bear your expenses. Just get to Springfield to meet us in early February. I'll let you know

exactly when and where, as soon as arrangements are completed."
"You'll like Thompson," he added. "He was the man most responsible for freeing the slaves in the British West Indies. He led the
antislavery fight in England that made their freedom possible."

Sojourner agreed to meet Garrison and Thompson in Springfield.

A Lecture Tour

TWENTY

ဢ Two months later, carpetbag bulging with copies of her *Narrative*, Sojourner Truth walked into the town of Springfield, Massachusetts. The mobs had got there before her. It was a freezing February day, yet roving bands of idle men could be seen everywhere in the streets. Several times she detoured around these bands of men as she moved toward the hotel where she was to meet Garrison.

She crossed the town square at dusk, and was startled to see three limp bodies hanging by their necks from a leafless tree, their legs jerking in the cold wind. Closer inspection revealed only three stuffed figures. She recognized the likeness of Wendell Phillips; the other two faces were strange to her.

On reaching the hotel, she asked for Garrison, only to be told, "Mr. Garrison is not expected." A tall, slender man stepped forward. She recognized the big features and thin, graying hair; they resembled those on one of the other stuffed figures outside. But the features on the figure dangling in the park had been twisted into a devil's leer. Here, as the man smiled at her, they seemed to radiate only the most pleasant, sincere warmth. It was George Thompson. He laughed about the effigies and explained that the third one must have been John Bull, the symbol of England. Then he told her that Garrison was ill and would not be able to join them on tour.

"Will you accept me as an escort in his place?"

She hesitated. "I have no money," she said. She would never have come if Garrison had not offered to pay her expenses.

"Never mind," Thompson said promptly. "I'll bear your expenses with pleasure." He took her arm to lead her to dinner.

"I was to give my first lecture tonight," he said, seating her at his right. "But I don't know yet whether Samuel May will find us a hall. It's proving more difficult than we had anticipated." Samuel May was a hard-working Unitarian minister and one of Garrison's staunchest friends.

"He will find a hall, if anyone can," Sojourner assured Thompson.

"All week long," Thompson continued, "the editors of this town have been urging the local people to mob me. The cotton mill workers have real reason to hate the English, of course. Most came here from Ireland because they were starving to death, and their English landlords would do nothing to help them at the time of the famine. Now the Springfield papers are telling the Irish that I've come over from England to free the slaves who'll then be free to take jobs away from the Irish—and the Irish will be as hungry in America as ever they were in Ireland. Naturally, that kind of talk isn't going to make them feel very friendly toward me."

Samuel May failed to find them a meeting hall that night. All evening Sojourner and Thompson listened to the mobs parading under their hotel windows. The fifes were blowing and the drums were banging, as if this were the army of the American Revolution, itself. The Irish were all set to drive the British back across the sea. But around eleven o'clock quiet fell. And by next morning, Reverend May even had a hall.

Thompson spoke there before lunch and again at night. And again the mobs were out with their fifes and drums. This time when the abolitionists returned to their hotel, they found flames licking the stuffed form of George Thompson that dangled from the lamppost outside the hotel. Dark figures in Indian headdress stomped and whirled around the burning effigy. As the dark-skinned woman and the white man stared through the hotel window, a rotten egg cracked against the pane. Another crack, and the window burst in a shower of glass particles, leaving a round gray cobblestone on the rug at Sojourner's feet.

They were preparing to move on to their next speaking engagement, the following morning, when a committee of citizens in top hats and tail coats was ushered hastily in to see Thompson. The committee had come to apologize. They were deeply distressed at the treatment accorded the English visitor. Would Mr. Thompson please not venture to judge the town of Springfield by the behavior of its ruffians?

Thompson stared coldly at the five prosperous-looking men. "Where were you last night, gentlemen? Respectable people like yourselves are the very ones responsible for this outrage. Your silence is the only thing that makes it possible. In fact, gentlemen, the so-called respectable people of Springfield—your editors and your politicians—are the very ones who incited the riot. No, I will not judge Springfield by its ruffians but by the true culprits—those who incited the ruffians and those who allowed it." He turned his back. "Good day, gentlemen."

As Sojourner Truth, George Thompson, and Samuel May drove away in their coach toward their next destination, May told of running into an Irish mob the previous afternoon.

"Where are you going?" he had asked.

The mob leader, flashing a cheerful smile, had replied, "To mob Thompson."

"Why?" asked Sam May.

"Because he is the enemy of Ireland."

May had been sincerely surprised. "The enemy of Ireland? How is that? Do you know he is one of the truest friends Ireland ever had in the English Parliament?"

The leader of the mob had held up one hand to halt his followers.

"No!" He had appeared astonished. "Is it so indeed?"

May had found it quite simple to persuade him. The leader had disbanded his men and all trotted cheerfully back in the direction from which they had come.

Thompson and Sojourner laughed heartily at this story.

It was a cold, rainy day. The coach and horses splashed continuously through muddy puddles as they rolled on through the bare February landscape of the Berkshire Hills toward New York State. At Union City, Little Falls, and West Winfield, they met friendly receptions. At Peterboro, they stayed with Gerrit Smith.

Smith was a wealthy New Yorker who had once been a large slaveowner, having inherited enormous properties in New York State from his father. But he firmly believed the state had failed in its responsibilities to its freed slaves, that Negroes had a right to own land, and in fact never could be truly free without land of their own. So he had taken one hundred and fifty thousand acres of his inheritance and cut it up into farms for three thousand Negro families whom he had invited to settle there. John Brown, a white farmer and storekeeper from Springfield, Massachusetts, had joined the colony, too, and was teaching the Negroes how to farm their land. This landowner was like none Sojourner Truth had ever met. She thought about him a great deal, as their carriage rolled along toward Syracuse the next morning.

The abolitionists spoke in Syracuse, and Sojourner was first on the program. The crowd screamed its displeasure. "Thompson, Thompson," they cried. Unperturbed, she raised her arms to quiet her audience.

"I'll tell you what Thompson is going to say to you," she shouted. "He's going to argue that the poor Negroes ought to be out of slavery and in the heavenly state of Freedom. But, children, I'm here to tell you that I'm against slavery because I want to keep the white folks who hold the slaves from getting sent straight to hell." Now they were listening.

When she had finished and sat down, she heard the crowd gasp in disbelief. Samuel May was moving forward, leading five fugitive slaves onto the platform. Everyone present knew that under the Fugitive Slave Bill, every fugitive was in constant danger of capture and return, and that every man who aided a fugitive was in equal danger of arrest. Yet there, standing confidently in front of the crowd, was Samuel May—pointing to four tired, ragged Negro men and a slender young woman.

"Men, matrons, and maidens of Syracuse," he cried. (For such a small man, he had a huge voice.) "See these victims of tyranny before you, and one of them a woman. I call on you to answer me now—shall these fugitives be taken from Syracuse?"

"NAY!" The answer was a roar soaring through the packed hall.

"Citizens of Syracuse," he shouted again. "Will you defend

with your lives, if need be, these defenseless and hunted children of God?"

"AYE!" Again a roar.

Now came the real question.

"Who will furnish them with employment?"

Who would dare? The employer of a fugitive was guilty of a crime under the bill and subject to a huge fine and imprisonment. Yet Sojourner saw people pushing forward to the platform, and within fifteen minutes, all five fugitives had jobs. Moreover their new employers had consented to having their own names publicly broadcast.

By mid-April—addressing antislavery audiences all the way— Thompson, May, and Sojourner Truth had worked their way up the entire chain of towns that flanked the Erie Canal, and had arrived in Rochester. Sojourner was seeing for the first time towns that had sprung up in New York during her own lifetime. But Rochester was the most interesting. People there claimed that houses were going up so fast the hens hardly had time to fly down from their roosts before a building went up over their heads. Others insisted that tree stumps could be found in the cellars of the most splendid buildings; there had been no time to uproot them.

The feel of the air was pleasing to Sojourner Truth. It came from across the lake, from Canada, where fugitives were safe. She also liked the people she met. They had a bustling, hard-working attitude. And Rochester was a strong antislavery town—probably because it always needed more cheap labor than it could get.

Frederick Douglass already had come to settle here and was publishing an antislavery paper, *The North Star.* "I know of no place where I could have located with less resistance or received a larger measure of cooperation," he wrote later.

Douglass headed the local branch of the Underground Railroad. One of the Railroad's principal routes ended at the docks on the Genesee River. From there regular steamers sailed down the river and across Lake Erie to Canada. Once aboard, any fugitive was safe; the steamers sailed under the protection of His Majesty, the King of England. No United States marshal could take a fugitive off. Thousands of men, women, and children were fleeing along this route to Canada. Many had escaped from the South years earlier and settled in northern communities. Now, the bill made their recapture possible at any moment.

George Thompson was scheduled to cross the border to speak in Canada. Sojourner decided to let him go on without her. People around Rochester were eager to hear an antislavery speaker. She decided she would stay for a while and satisfy that eagerness.

At her first Rochester meeting Sojourner had met a shy-looking woman with mousy brown hair who had invited her to stay with her husband and herself. Amy and Isaac Post were well known local abolitionists. Sojourner had recognized immediately the thee and thou of their soft Quaker speech. But Isaac told her, "We are no longer Quakers. Quakers are not firm enough in their fight against slavery."

Sojourner stayed with the Posts throughout the early months of spring. Amy escorted her to many meetings. The shy little woman would sit quietly knitting while her tall friend rose to speak or moved through the audience selling her *Narrative*. Afterward, they would clamber back into Amy's carriage and return to the house on Sophia Street.

Several times at night, while staying with the Posts, Sojourner was awakened by the sound of horses' hooves. When she went to her window, she saw the Post's carriage moving swiftly toward the gate, curtains tightly drawn. She did not need to inquire where the carriage was headed. It was pointed toward Buell Avenue and the docks along the Genesee. Isaac Post had underground passengers to deliver. One morning Amy Post proudly confided, "We had twelve of them in the barn last night." Sojourner knew very well who "them" meant. Amy's plain face glowed with satisfaction. "That's the most we ever had," she said, her needles clicking swiftly as she picked up the stitches.

Sojourner Truth made many good friends in Rochester. The rough frontier spirit of western New York suited her, and she felt her testimony was well received at the meetings she attended. But when she heard talk of antislavery conventions coming up in Ohio, her spirit again grew restless. Was the Lord giving her a signal—pointing her west now, just as eight years earlier he had said to a servant called Isabelle, "Go east"?

She decided he was. In May she bade the Posts good-bye. All alone now, the tall old woman boarded the steamer for Detroit. There was to be a Woman's Rights Convention in Akron. If Sojourner Truth knew anything about the woman's rights movement, she knew she would be the only Negro woman there, and that she would be needed.

And Aren't I a Woman?

T W E N T Y O N E

౨ Nervous whispers passed among the listeners in the Akron
Church when Sojourner Truth appeared in the aisle. Her gaunt
body was topped by a floppy sunbonnet, which covered her white
turban.

"I told you so."

"An abolitionist affair."

"Woman's rights and Negroes'."

The audience at the Woman's Rights Convention included
many midwestern housewives who were not at all sure they might
not have done far better to stay home. The sight of this powerful-

looking woman in a long black gown only confirmed their worst fears. Since there was not an empty seat left in the church, Sojourner strode unhesitatingly toward the pulpit and planted herself on the step. She sat there, a silent listener, elbows resting on her knees, chin on both broad, calloused palms. From the shadow of the sunbonnet, her deep eyes intently studied the uptilted faces. During intermission she moved quietly about, selling her *Narrative*.

Several hours passed. Sojourner noticed that the bolder women were beginning to speak up more firmly, while the more timid ones seemed to be wondering what had ever possessed them to come in the first place. The sight of Sojourner quietly watching from the pulpit kept these more timid ones in a state of constant nervous flutter. At last several of them ran over to the large, vigorous chairman.

"Mrs. Gage, please don't let that Negro woman speak. It will ruin us. Every newspaper in the land will have our cause mixed up with abolition, and we shall be utterly denounced."

Frances Gage was an old antislavery fighter, married to a man who felt just as she did about slavery and woman's rights. She could afford to smile. No matter what the papers reported, she had no worry about what her husband would say when she got home. She replied soothingly, "We shall see when the time comes."

On the second day of the convention, ministers suddenly appeared from all four corners of Ohio. Everyone present knew that these gentlemen had not traveled such a distance over dirt roads for nothing. As the day grew hotter, the general apprehension grew. At last, a portly gentleman stood up in his pew, sweat rolling over the edge of his clerical collar. "Of course the Lord intended man to have superior rights and privileges," he boomed. "Did the Lord not make his intellect superior to that of woman?"

A second man, as hungry-looking as the first had been well fed, picked up the argument. "Was not Christ a man?" he shouted. "Would God not, at that time, have given some token of his wish to have women equal? If indeed he had wished such a thing!"

A third minister shook a bony clerical finger. "According to the Bible, it was not man but woman who sinned by accepting the apple from the serpent. Was not that a proof of God's wish to make her inferior?"

As Frances Gage reported later, "There were very few women in those days who dared speak in meeting." Some women appeared almost to cower in their pews. Others, stung by the sneers of a group of idle bystanders, were flushed with anger. For a moment Mrs. Gage feared the entire convention would break into tears and hysterics.

Her thoughts were interrupted by a gasp of horror. Sojourner was slowly rising to her feet. "For God's sake, Mrs. Gage, *don't* let her speak!" Mrs. Gage's neighbor whispered loudly.

Sojourner seemed not to have heard. She advanced to the front of the audience, slowly took off her sunbonnet, and laid it at her feet. Her large eyes turned toward Frances Gage, seeking permission. The chairman raised her hand to interrupt the hiss sweeping the pews. "Sojourner Truth," she announced quietly.

Every woman present appeared to be holding her breath, as all eyes fastened on the tall, straight-backed figure before the altar. Sojourner's voice was not loud, but as always, its resonance carried her words to every ear in the house. "Well, children," she began, "where there is so much racket, there must be somethin' out of kilter. I think between the Negroes of the South and the women of the North—all talkin' about rights—the white men will be in a fix pretty soon. But what's all this about anyway?

"That man over there." Her long finger shot toward the minister in question. "He says women need to be helped into car-

riages and lifted over ditches and to have the best everywhere."
She smiled, shaking her head gently. "Nobody ever helps me into
carriages, over mud puddles, or gets me any best place."

To Frances Gage, the woman standing on the pulpit steps
seemed a giant among pygmies, towering over the crowded
pews.

"Aren't I a woman?" Sojourner cried out. "Look at me!" She
bared her powerful right arm and raised it high in the air. "Look
at my arm. I have ploughed. And I have planted. And I have
gathered into barns. And no man could head me. *And aren't I a
woman?*

"I could work as much," she continued, "and eat as much as
any man—when I could get it—and bear the lash as well. And
aren't I a woman? I have borne children and seen them sold into
slavery, and when I cried out with a mother's grief, none but
Jesus heard me. *And aren't I a woman?*"

Her finger pointed to another minister. "He talks about this
thing in the head." She hesitated, looking around at the women
nearest her. "What's that they call it?" she asked.

"Intellect," whispered the woman nearest the podium.

"That's it, honey," Sojourner nodded approvingly, and turning
back to the audience continued. "What's intellect got to do with
women's rights or black folks' rights? If my cup won't hold but a
pint, and yours holds a quart, wouldn't you be mean not to let me
have my little half-measure full?"

The women in the audience were stirring with delight.

"That little man in black there! He says women can't have as
much rights as men, 'cause Christ wasn't a woman." Her arms
stretched wide as if to evoke the cross, and her eyes burned.
"Where did your Christ come from?

"Where did he come from?" Her question rolled over the

packed, silent pews. "From God and a woman." She looked witheringly at the minister in question. "Man had nothing to do with him."

Now, with a twinkle, she turned her attention back to the women. "If the first woman God ever made was strong enough to turn the world upside down all alone, these women together ought to be able to turn it back and get it right-side up again. And now that they are asking to do it, the men better let 'em." She stooped over to pick up her sunbonnet. "Obliged to you for hearin' me," she said sweetly.

In August she was reported in Salem, Ohio, at the Anniversary Convention of the Antislavery Society. She was seen in the middle of the front row, listening intently to Frederick Douglass. His eyes, that day, flashed with angry despair as he spoke of the suffering of thousands of Negro men, women, and children crossing the Ohio River, fleeing toward Canada—only to be caught and returned to the South. His voice choked as he spoke of the men in both North and South, who profited from a system that brought so much human misery. "There is no longer any hope for justice other than bloody rebellion," he cried. "Slavery must end in blood."

The silence that followed these words was overpowering. Even an abolitionist crowd, in those years, was not accustomed to such strong ideas. They sat stunned. Then a voice broke the silence, a voice almost as deep as Douglass's own. Sojourner Truth had risen to her feet, her arm pointed accusingly at the famous editor of *The North Star.*

"Frederick," she paused. "Frederick, is God dead?"

"No," Douglass answered quickly. "And because God is not dead, slavery can only end in blood."

But not many people were yet prepared to accept this new, more fiery abolitionist creed. Certainly not Sojourner. Hers was still a God of peace. She continued on her road, testifying in her own way, preferring to start her own meetings and whenever people would buy, selling her *Narrative*.

Ohio

TWENTY TWO

&❧ In 1851, the Underground Railroad ran in a maze through the state of Ohio. A spur started at almost every town on the Ohio River. The river was the barrier that separated the free state of Ohio from the slaveholding state of Kentucky. But for those who escaped across the river and the abolitionists who helped them, Ohio was not really so free. True, the Underground Railroad had two conductors for every mile of "track" within the state. But many Ohio citizens sympathized with slavery, and state laws still made the work of antislavery men dangerous and difficult.

For years Ohio had had a law requiring a certificate of freedom

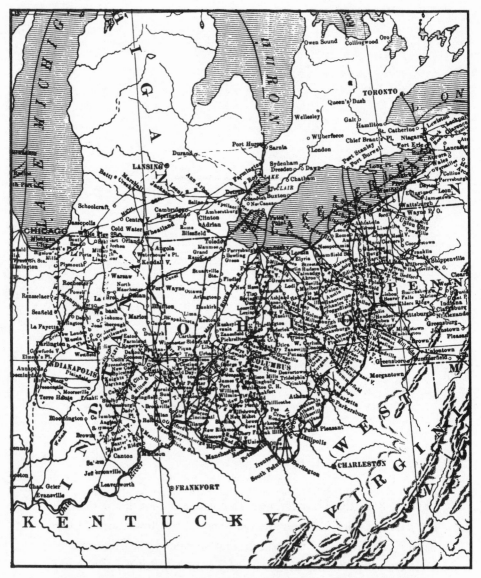

A maze of underground routes passed through Ohio in the years before and during the Civil War. This map is taken from The Underground Railroad by W. H. Siebert, published in 1898.

for every Negro who settled in the state. In 1829 the state had even passed its own Fugitive Slave Law. It had its "Black Laws" too—laws that applied only to Negroes and restricted their movements in many ways.

Sojourner felt certain that if Ohio folk understood more clearly what slavery really was, more of them would be fighting against it. Her testimony, she thought, could be helpful here in softening up the people and in making more of them friendly to the underground.

Friends in Salem, Ohio, loaned her a horse and buggy, and she loaded in six hundred copies of her *Narrative* that had been forwarded to her by Garrison. Next to these she laid a furled-up white satin banner that the ladies had presented to her after the Akron Woman's Rights Convention. Across the white silk, printed in bold black letters was the legend "Proclaim liberty throughout all the land unto all the inhabitants thereof."

For two years, Sojourner's high-wheeled borrowed buggy lurched over the rutted Ohio roads, traveling up and down the land as the Lord seemed to instruct her. She became a familiar sight in many a country town. A tall, witty, wise old black woman, telling whomever would listen of the wrongs inflicted on her people.

Ohio was large. Towns and villages lay far apart. Sojourner could ride for hours sometimes without passing a single farmhouse or even reaching a crossing. Narrow dirt roads wandered over rolling hills, through mile after mile of uncut forest. Slopes lay dark in the sun, as densely covered with trees as the Catskills of her childhood.

Chicks and hogs roaming the muddy streets of small rural towns reminded her of Ulster County, too. But here houses were frequently only log cabins: two or three rooms and a fireplace, with perhaps a ladder leading up to a loft. And the people she met in rural Ohio were as plain as their homes, plain-speaking and dressed in simple, coarse clothing. Sojourner enjoyed matching wits with them.

When she set out in the morning, she as often as not flicked the reins with no special destination in mind. Reaching a crossroads, she would drop the reins on the horse's neck. "God," she would pray, "you drive." And, she insisted later, God always did drive her to some good place where she could have a successful meeting and her horse would be well fed and watered.

Her singing always attracted a crowd. She would stop at a likely-looking crossing where farm families passed on their way to market, or in the muddy public square of some rural village. The white satin banner would be unfurled, its pole planted in the dust.

> *It was early in the morning,*
> *It was early in the morning,*
> *Just at the break of day,*
> *When He rose, when He rose, when He rose,*
> *And went to heaven on a cloud.*

The voice would soar above the flapping patch of shiny white cloth and the hymns she sang were often as familiar to her frontier listeners as the sampler on their wall embroidered "Home, Sweet Home." But her voice turned any hymn into something rich and strange, full of bright threads and unexpected colors. People who understood nothing of the life of Sojourner Truth, and cared neither one way nor the other about slavery, listened and were moved.

As the voice drifted through the clear air above the fresh-turned soil of spring fields or the brown dust of village streets, doors popped open and women appeared, heavy babies straddling their hips, hands damp from the washtub. Men left their plows and came in from the fields. A passing farmer reined in his horse and sat listening, with three solemn-faced children seated next to him on the wagon bench.

As she reached the end of her song, Sojourner's keen eyes would peer speculatively over the gold rims of her spectacles. "Now children . . ." She was never sure until she was well along in her testimony whether the crowd was antislavery or not. Feeling, one way or the other, ran high in Ohio. Yet she never worried about the safety of her person. She was always certain that God was present as her bodyguard. Had he not personally sent her here to testify?

One day a heckler tried his luck arguing with Sojourner. "Is it not true," he asked, "that the United States Constitution has not a single word in it against slavery? Are you attacking the Constitution, old woman?"

Sojourner looked thoughtfully past her questioner.

That year, in Ohio, a tiny beetle called a weevil had ruined the wheat crop. The beetle was so tiny that it could crawl right inside a husk and hollow out the grain. "Children," she said now. "I talks to God and God talks to me. I goes out and talks to God in the fields and in the woods. This morning I was walkin' out, and I climbed over a fence. I saw the wheat holdin' up its head, lookin' so big. I goes up and takes hold of it." Her voice dropped to a whisper. "Would you believe it? *There was no wheat there!* I says, 'God, what's the matter with this wheat?' And he says to me, 'Sojourner, there's a little weevil in it.'"

She cocked her head. "Now I hears talk about the Constitution and the rights of man. I comes up and I takes hold of this Constitution. It looks mighty big. And I feels for my rights. But they ain't there. Then I says, 'God, what ails this Constitution?' And you know what he says to me? God says, 'Sojourner, there's a little weevil in it.'"

Another day, her horse and buggy rolled up to an antislavery convention in Ashtabula County. Sojourner's bushy-bearded old friend Parker Pillsbury was the chief speaker and the audience appeared sympathetic.

But suddenly a young law student sprang to his feet, shouting, "Negroes are fit only to be slaves. Why if any one of them ever shows so much as a spark of intelligence, you may be sure that spark was ignited by white blood flowing in his veins. As a race the Negro is only a connecting link between men and animals." He rambled on for fully an hour, while the audience stirred with annoyance.

Suddenly clouds blotted out the sun. Thunder crashed and a driving sheet of water flattened the grass outside. Branches snapped from trees and battered the sides of the meeting hall. In the dark, not even the faces on the platform could be distinguished.

The young lawyer stood trembling in the silenced hall. "It is the voice of God!" he cried. "The lightning you see is the flash of his Almighty Eye, enraged that you dare hold such meetings and preach such doctrines. I am almost afraid to be in your company."

At that moment, a tall form emerged from the gloom, dressed in dark green, the crossed corners of a white kerchief gleaming on her breast. A white turban crowned the woman's head, and her white teeth and eyeballs glistened in the shadows. Between bursts of thunder came her voice—calm, subdued, and serene.

"When I was a slave, away down there in New York and there was any particularly bad work to be done, some colored woman was sure to be called on to do it. And when I heard that man talkin' away there as he did, almost a whole hour, I said to myself, here's one spot of work sure that's just fit for colored folk to clean up after. I'm going to reply to this critter." She leaned forward, as if to peer better into the eyes of her audience. "Now, children," she asked. "Don't you pity me, having to do such scullion work?"

A burst of thunder drowned the laughter that filled the hall. She waited for both to subside. Then she straightened herself proudly.

"I am the pure African. You can all see that plain enough. None of your white blood runs in my veins." Another tremendous peal of thunder drowned out her voice. The young lawyer was trembling like a leaf about to be torn from its tree.

"You're afraid the Lord has sent the storm in wrath at our opinions?" she asked him, leaning forward solicitously, as if to comfort a very small creature. "Child, don't be scared. You're not goin' to be harmed. Why I don't expect God's even heard about you yet."

She was climbing back into her wagon one day after a meeting, when a man caught hold of her horse's bridle. "Old woman, do you think your talk about slavery does any good? Do you suppose people care what you say? Why I don't care any more for your talk than I do for the bite of a flea."

She looked at him, good naturedly. "Perhaps not," she replied, flicking the reins as she clucked to her horse. "Perhaps not. But, the Lord willing, I'll keep you scratchin'!"

She did indeed "keep them scratchin'" in Ohio, singing her songs and talking religion and abolition all the way. In order to pay her costs, she sold her homemade songs and her shadows. And she managed to dispose of so many copies of her *Narrative* that by the end of her journey she was able to pay Sam Hill every penny she owed on the little house in Northampton.

In 1853, after more than two years, Sojourner Truth returned her borrowed horse and buggy, discarded the floppy sunbonnet, and headed for home.

Return

TWENTY THREE

ॐ She discovered that she could travel by train now from Rochester to New York. The laying of tracks had been completed along the Erie Canal to Albany and down along the Hudson to the sea. She bought a ticket, but found she must sit in the smoker.

"No colored person allowed in the coach," said the conductor.

Sojourner didn't mind a little smoke. She had puffed a pipe herself since her slavery days. But she would have preferred another reason for being ordered to sit in the smoker. A few years later, when a friend urged her to give up her pipe, she replied, "No. I have been sent into so many smoking cars, I smoke now in self-defense. I would much rather swallow my own smoke than another's."

She paused to address the Woman's Rights Convention in session in New York. But she did not stay long. She wanted to see her daughters. Diana still lived in New Paltz. Elizabeth lived in Connecticut. She was Elizabeth Banks now, with a three-year-old son named Sammy. Hannah, already widowed, was the mother of a nine-year-old boy named James Caldwell.

As, one by one, Sojourner visited with her girls and their children, her old longing to gather them close around her returned. But after her experiences in Ohio, she doubted that she really wanted to live in the East. She had found herself far more at home in the West, among plain-speaking people who were only a step removed from the pioneers.

She spoke to her daughters of towns in Ohio or Michigan where a fugitive slave was almost as safe as in Canada or England. Battle Creek, for instance. A conductor on the Underground Railroad could escort his passenger down the main street of a town like that with a brass band and hallelujah chorus, it was said, and never worry about slave catchers.

"Battle Creek? I've heard of that town. Several families from New Paltz and Kingston moved out there even before I left Ulster County," Hannah said. "Now James's pa's dead, I been thinking of going there myself with my boy. I hear there's plenty of jobs in Michigan. And the schools take Negro children."

After a few days of visiting, Sojourner was ready to continue north toward Massachusetts. "Why don't you let me take James with me for company?" she asked Hannah. "I'll bring him back in a week or two." Her daughter agreed, and James set off in great excitement with his grandmother. But the two did not go immediately to Northampton. One of Sojourner's secret reasons for returning east had been to pay an important call.

While in Ohio, she had heard a great deal of talk about a new book that everyone was reading. Like Sojourner's own book, this one was written by a woman and spoke out strongly against slavery. But the author of this new book was an educated white woman.

Bookstores were eager to display it. Already it had been translated into several foreign languages and even made into a play that was playing to packed houses when Sojourner passed through New York.

The new book was called *Uncle Tom's Cabin*. A friend in Ohio had read Sojourner several chapters and asked for her opinion. She thought it was a good book. But she wondered why the author thought a Negro had to have light skin to be intelligent. Only the light-skinned slaves in the book seemed to have any brains at all. Nevertheless, Sojourner knew the lady had struck a hard blow against slavery. She was anxious to meet her.

One day, holding little James Caldwell by the hand, Sojourner Truth lifted the brass knocker on the door of a large stone house in Andover. The old lady and the small boy sat patiently in the handsomely furnished downstairs hall of the house until Harriet Beecher Stowe came down. Sojourner rose. For a long moment, the tall woman who had been a slave and struggled so desperately for her rights looked down at this tiny woman who had always lived a protected, sheltered life.

"So this is you," she said at last.

"Yes," said Harriet.

Harriet Stowe had her father and several clergymen staying with her that week. All of them became so interested in talking to Sojourner that they persuaded her to stay for several days. Nine years later, Harriet Stowe told about this visit and the impression Sojourner Truth made on all of them in an article she wrote for *The Atlantic Monthly*. Many of the things we know today about Sojourner's early life come from this article.

War in the West

TWENTY FOUR

&⟨ In 1856 Sojourner Truth moved to Battle Creek, Michigan. By that time, the center of the antislavery struggle had shifted to the midwestern states where she felt so at home. Now she knew even more surely that she belonged in the West and not in the East.

The shift in the center of the struggle between slave and free states had started in 1854 when Congress had passed the Kansas-Nebraska Bill. This new bill revoked the earlier Missouri Compromise, which had been so bitterly opposed by the abolitionists but excused by many politicians who insisted it would be a final compromise with slavery. The Kansas-Nebraska Bill threw out the borderline between free and slave territory so firmly drawn by that earlier bill. The new bill said in effect: let the settlers themselves decide. If they want a future state to be slave, let it be slave. If they want it free, let it be free. Whether a state lies north or south of the Missouri Line, leave the question of slavery strictly up to the settlers themselves.

A howl rose up in the northern states. And it was not only the shouts of angry abolitionists. All men who believed in free labor were outraged. Men with initiative were needed to develop the West, not slaves with no reason to work except the lash. In the Midwest, a new party called the Republican Party was founded on a single issue: no extension of slavery.

The territory whose immediate future was at stake was Kansas. How could free labor men get settlers into Kansas before slavery men outnumbered them in the vote?

Emigrant societies, hastily formed in New England, recruited farmers and shipped them West in wagons and in boats with plows strapped to the decks. But the South had the advantage; its settlers had only to cross the border from Missouri. Men shook their heads grimly. There would be bloodshed, they said, before the matter was settled.

In 1856 a local war erupted. Missourians burned the Kansas town of Lawrence to the ground, and Gerrit Smith's friend John Brown, with the help of his five strapping sons, struck back against the proslavery settlers at Pottawatomie Creek. For years, John Brown had been saying that the only way to pry loose the grip of the slaveowner was by arming the slaves and helping them to rebel. Now, in 1857, a decision of the United States Supreme Court forced many other abolitionists to the same conclusion.

The decision concerned a slave called Dred Scott who had been taken by his master into territory where slavery was illegal. When the master started to return home, the slave had claimed his freedom and refused to accompany him. But the Court ruled that Congress had no authority to abolish slavery in any of the territories. Moreover, the Court said, no Negro had rights any white man need respect.

There were dissenters in the Court, of course, just as there were antislavery fighters in the proslavery Congress. But every branch of the American government now appeared solidly in the grip of men who wanted slavery. More and more, people were asking, "Can such a grip be broken by peaceable means?" But others, including Sojourner Truth and many abolitionists who followed Garrison, felt there was still a way to avoid bloodshed. The problem was to engage more people in the antislavery struggle, persuade thousands more that slavery was wrong, until at last the government would be forced to listen.

From her new home in Battle Creek, Sojourner traveled into Indiana on a speaking tour with her old friend from New England, Parker Pillsbury. Indiana was a rough place for abolitionists. The rolling hills and rich black earth had attracted many settlers from the South. More than once hecklers made it impossible for the tall old Negro woman and the stocky black-bearded ex-minister to hold their meetings.

In Kosciusko County, a rumor was circulated that Sojourner was an impostor, a man disguised in women's clothing. A large number of proslavery people turned up at one of the meetings. Their leader, a local doctor, had bet forty dollars that Sojourner was a man. Just as she started to speak, he stepped forward, hands raised above his head.

"Hold on," he shouted. "There is strong doubt in the minds of many persons here regarding the sex of the next speaker. A majority of us in fact are convinced that the speaker is not a woman but a man disguised as a woman. For the speaker's own sake, we

This photograph of Sojourner Truth was taken sometime during the years she first traveled through the Midwest. A crippled forefinger can be seen on her right hand, perhaps from the scythe cut she received during her last year with John Dumont.

demand, if it be a she, that she expose her breast to the gaze of some of the ladies present so that they may report back and dispel the audience's doubts."

Sojourner noticed many of the women flushing with embarrassment and anger at the man's suggestion. Pillsbury, who was hearing the rumor for the first time, strode quickly toward the doctor. His hand was raised and his face above the square black beard was crimson. Sojourner feared he would hurl the doctor to the ground. She rose hastily.

"Why do you suppose me to be a man?"

"Your voice is not the voice of a woman," replied the doctor. "It is the voice of a man and we believe that you are a man." He turned to face the audience and called out, "Let's put the matter to a vote. Is this person a man?"

The crowd roared "Aye."

Quietly, her fingers steady, Sojourner began to untie the white kerchief across her breast. Slowly her hands moved to undo the buttons at the top of her dress.

"I will show my breast," she announced as the last button came undone, "but to the entire congregation." And as she opened her blouse, she added with slow emphasis, "It is not my shame but yours that I do this."

Sojourner was past sixty now. But this was no time for an antislavery fighter to rest. Alone, she pushed into Illinois and Ohio and traveled throughout Michigan, gathering listeners wherever she could by her singing and her testifying.

The arguments about slavery were growing sharper. Tempers frayed easily. Insults were backed up by tomatoes and eggs and sometimes even rocks. In Kansas both sides were murdering men as they slept in their beds. Then in 1859 John Brown drove the antislavery war—because already it was a war—onto southern territory. October 16, 1859, with a handful of followers, he raided the federal arsenal at Harpers Ferry, Virginia.

The fierce-eyed prophet had hoped to seize the guns stored in that arsenal and distribute them among slaves. He failed. As he lay wounded in the courtroom, awaiting trial, John Brown explained why he had defied the federal government: "I pity the poor in bondage that have none to help them. That is why I am here. . . . It is my sympathy with the oppressed and wronged who are as good as you and as precious in the sight of God. . . . Had I interfered in behalf of the rich, the powerful, the intelligent, or the so-called great, every man in this court would have deemed it an act worthy of reward rather than punishment."

The day after Harpers Ferry, angry white mobs marched through the streets of Battle Creek in support of John Brown. Crowds were marching in all the cities of the northern and western states. In Boston even Sojourner's friend Garrison, who had always opposed violence as a means of freeing the slaves, now cried, "In firing his gun, John Brown has merely told us what time it is. It is high noon, thank God!"

Another friend of Sojourner's New England days stood over Brown's body as it was lowered into its Adirondack Mountain grave. "John Brown," said Wendell Phillips, "has loosened the roots of the slave system. It only breathes—it does not live— hereafter."

The following year disgusted voters swept out the old parties and elected the candidate of the new Republican Party, Abraham Lincoln, President of the United States.

Who was this Abraham Lincoln? Sojourner Truth had never heard his name before. But the South knew who he was. It had warned what it would do if Lincoln were elected. Now it carried out its threat. One month after the election, South Carolina seceded from the Union. Other states quickly followed. By April

1861 southern cannon were firing on the federal defenses at Fort Sumter, off Charleston Harbor. The South was in open rebellion. The war over slavery had officially begun.

Sojourner Truth was tired. Her limbs ached from the long years of traveling up and down the land, trying to make people see the truth about slavery, always believing, as Garrison had, that slavery could and must end without violence. But with this war, even more than her body, her soul was tired. Despite her best efforts and those of others who had argued and talked as she had argued and talked, the time of violence had come, a time of terrible suffering for many men. And to what end? President Lincoln said he had no intention of interfering with slavery where it already existed. He said he had only sworn to prevent its spread. The administration in Washington felt that many northerners who were willing to fight to preserve the Union would never fight were the war to become one to free the slaves.

Blood was being shed, but no great changes were intended for Sojourner's people. This was not her fight. Better to rest from her wandering and await new instructions from the Lord. She knew she would not mind this time if his message took a little longer than usual to reach her.

Meanwhile, there were good things in her life. For the first time since her slavery days, Sojourner was actually gathering her family around her. Her daughter Elizabeth and her grandson Sammy Banks were now living with her in her house in Battle Creek. Sammy was in school learning to read and write. James Caldwell lived with her, too—a handsome seventeen-year-old.

When she was not out lecturing, Sojourner earned her living as she always had. She cooked, cleaned, took in laundry, and cared for the sick. She was a greatly respected citizen of Battle Creek and had many friends there. Her employers generally were antislavery people who were proud to have her working for them and made her a welcome guest at their table.

Sometimes, in summer, she could be seen striding along the streets of the town, a tray of purple berries crowning her turban. A Quaker friend, Charles Merritt, owned a huge blackberry patch and let her sell the fruit. The day before she was to pass, her grandson Sammy would distribute handbills along Sojourner's route to warn the housewives she was coming. It was worth waiting to buy from Sojourner Truth. There were no plumper, blacker, juicier berries than Charles Merritt's and the old Negro woman's stories of her life and her antislavery adventures made the quiet day memorable.

Meanwhile, far away, the cannons continued to roar. And now, despite Mr. Lincoln's caution, despite those northerners who would "never fight to free the slaves," people began to notice that increasing numbers of slaves were, in fact, being freed. What, for instance, was to be done with the thousands of slaves fleeing into the Union ranks? Returning them would only help the Confederacy. In New Orleans, General Ben Butler hit on a practical solution. He called the fugitives "contraband of war" and put them to work building fortifications and growing food for the Union Army. The word "contraband" usually referred to materials an enemy could use for fighting a war. If the federal army called a slave "contraband" it was not arguing the rights and wrongs of slavery. On the other hand, it was unlikely that men who had helped the federal army would ever be returned to masters who had fought against that army.

In those first two years of war, there were other indications that this conflict would mark the end of the slavery system. One year after the guns opened fire on Fort Sumter, Lincoln signed a paper emancipating all slaves in the District of Columbia. Only five months later, the President issued a solemn warning: *All slaves in any state still in rebellion by January 1, 1863, would, as of that date, be free.*

Sojourner Truth, living peacefully in Battle Creek, was beginning to feel this might be her struggle after all; and having reached that conclusion, she began looking for a way to join it. As usual, it did not take her long to find what she wanted.

One brisk October day, she returned home to find an old friend sitting in her front parlor. Her visitor was Josephine Griffing, a widow with three daughters whom Sojourner had known in Ohio where Josephine had been one of the most stubborn of the antislavery fighters. More than once during those years, this delicate-looking little woman had slipped alone through dark fields at night, hoping to avoid the tar pot. Once she had passed close enough for her nostrils to itch from the pungent smell of the black mess heating in an iron kettle.

Today, Josephine Griffing wasted no time. "Sojourner," she said. "I've come once again to beg your help. As you know, the President has promised to free the slaves the first of the coming year. The war has indeed become what we dreamed it might—a war to end slavery. But the war effort is not going well. Many northerners openly oppose it. Others secretly sympathize with the rebellion. People must be made to understand the importance of helping our Union forces. Antislavery speakers are needed more than ever before to rally people to our cause. I have been asked to go into Indiana, and I want you to come with me."

Sojourner Truth rose without a word and went into the next room to get ready.

The carriage with the two women sped swiftly past the gently rolling fields and autumn colors of southern Michigan and across the border into Indiana. Oaks and beeches turned the low hills brown and red and gold between the patches of china-blue water.

As they jolted along, Josephine Griffing explained the situation in more detail. "Governor Morton of Indiana supports the President strongly. But proslavery men—Copperheads—control the Indiana legislature and, as you know, the people of the state are a mixed bag. There are secret organizations working there to obstruct the draft and doing everything they can to help the Confederates." She turned away. Her fine profile, for a moment, was etched against the carriage window.

"As I told you earlier, Sojourner, you must realize that this trip will be more dangerous for you than for me. The legislature has passed a law forbidding any Negro even to enter the state. The law, of course, is unconstitutional, but we are risking physical harm by challenging it at this time. Yet we must challenge it. There is never a right time to challenge a wrong law. And anything we can do to bolster Governor Morton will greatly help the war effort in Indiana."

Every turn of the wheels seemed to lift another pound of weariness from the soul of Sojourner Truth. She was back in harness, back at the work she loved best.

Two miles across the Indiana border the wheels ground to a stop. Men on horseback blocked the road. "The Negro woman is under arrest. She'll have to come with us."

There was nothing to do but obey. The carriage with the two women rolled slowly behind the mounted posse until they came to a courthouse. The group stopped at the door. Without even glancing at the mounted and armed men, five-foot Josephine Griffing leaped down from the carriage to find the judge. Five minutes later, she was out with judge at her elbow. "Let the old woman go," he snapped at the deputy.

Josephine Griffing climbed back into the carriage, still bristling. "He knew very well the law was unconstitutional," she said angrily. "And when he saw I knew it as well as he and was not to be bullied, there was nothing for him to do but to let you go." She smiled at Sojourner. "Sometimes," she said, "an educated woman who does not know her place is more effective in getting her way than a man." The wagon rolled on.

The two had been warned that armed men would be present at their first meeting, "ready to blow out your brains." They decided to hold the meeting anyway, but soon realized it was very little use; no one could hear a word they said. Hecklers peppered the air with shouts.

"The niggers have caused enough trouble."

"Stop your mouth and get out."

Boos, catcalls, and jeers drowned out the women's voices. Sojourner sternly wagged her finger at her hecklers and, peering solemnly over the rims of her spectacles, announced that she had no intention whatsoever of stopping up her mouth and that the Union people would soon enough make the hecklers stop up theirs if they didn't watch out. She gasped as a man grabbed her arm. Then she noticed his Union uniform. It was the Union home guard who had decided to take her into custody rather than risk another arrest.

Escorted by the guard, Sojourner and Josephine Griffing proceeded to Angola, near the Michigan border. A meeting was scheduled to be held in the town hall. Again the women were warned. "The Copperheads will burn the building to the ground."

"Then," answered Sojourner, "I will speak upon the ashes."

She said later, "The Union ladies of Angola thought I should be dressed in uniform as well as the captain of the home guard whose prisoner I was and who was to go with me to the meeting. So the ladies gave me a red, white, and blue shawl, a sash and apron to match, a cap on my head with a star in front, and a star on each shoulder. When I was dressed I looked in the glass and was fairly frightened. Said I, 'It seems I am going to battle.'

"My friends advised me to take a sword or a pistol. I replied, 'I carry no weapon. The Lord will preserve me without weapons. I feel safe even in the midst of my enemies, for the truth is all-powerful and will prevail.' Well, they put me in a splendid carriage and the home guard escorted me. When the rebels saw such a mighty army coming, they fled. By the time we arrived they were scattered over the fields, like a flock of frightened crows. Not one was left but a small boy upon the fence crying 'nigger.'"

For the first time since they had crossed the border into Indiana, Sojourner was able to speak without interruption. But their luck did not hold. At the next town, her host was arrested for

A broadside used by Sojourner to advertise her lectures.
COURTESY UNIVERSITY OF MICHIGAN COLLECTIONS

FREE LECTURE!

SOJOURNER TRUTH,

Who has been a slave in the State of New York, and who has been a Lecturer for the last twenty-three years, whose characteristics have been so vividly portrayed by Mrs. Harriet Beecher Stowe, as the African Sybil, will deliver a lecture upon the present issues of the day,

At   On

And will give her experience as a Slave mother and religious woman. She comes highly recommended as a public speaker, having the approval of many thousands who have heard her earnest appeals, among whom are Wendell Phillips, Wm. Lloyd Garrison, and other distinguished men of the nation.

☞ At the close of her discourse she will offer for sale her photograph and a few of her choice songs.

allowing a Negro under his roof. A second friend was hauled off to jail for encouraging her to stay. Again, both gentlemen were released when they refused to be intimidated.

The next day Sojourner was resting from her energetic campaign when a carriage rolled up to the house in a whirl of dust and two breathless ladies tumbled out. "Sojourner," they insisted, "you must hide in the woods immediately. The rebels will be here any minute."

Sojourner felt she would rather march to jail like a soldier than tremble like a rabbit in the underbrush. She had come to Indiana to fight for her right to speak, not to run off in panic.

A rebel constable galloped up, shortly after, with a warrant for her arrest. But right behind him was a Union officer, with another warrant—to take Sojourner into protective custody. The rebel constable whirled his horse around in disgust. "I'm not going to bother anymore with this kind of nonsense. I'd rather resign first," he shouted as he disappeared down the road.

As the tour continued, attempts to stop Sojourner grew increasingly feeble. On her last arrest, half the townspeople escorted her to her trial, shouting, "Sojourner, Free Speech, and the Union."

The court officials who had not expected either the prisoner or the crowd, irritably hunted up a room. After a while, two half-drunk lawyers tottered in the door, eyed the large group for a long moment, then tottered away and, as the crowd watched, entered a tavern across the street. That ended the trial.

Josephine Griffing wrote a report on this trip for the *National Anti-Slavery Standard* in New York: "Our meetings are largely attended by persons from every part of the county. Especially by the most noble-hearted women, whose presence has produced a marked impression and has done much toward establishing a free government. . . . The lines are now being drawn. . . . Slavery had made a conquest in this country by the suppression of free speech, and freedom must make her conquest by the steadfast support of free speech. There are a hundred men now who would spill their blood sooner than surrender the rights of Sojourner."

The Antislavery President

TWENTY FIVE

ટ~ Later that same year a rumor spread among Sojourner's friends back East: Sojourner Truth was dead.

It was not true. But she had exhausted herself in Indiana, and on her return to Battle Creek, she fell so ill that, for the first time in her sixty-five years, she could not care for herself. Afterward she always claimed that it was her friends and Mr. Lincoln who had saved her.

The Merritt family, whom she had so often helped when a member of that family was sick, insisted on taking her into their home to care for her. In New York, the *Anti-Slavery Standard*, whose editor, Oliver Johnson, had known her in Ohio, published an appeal for help. Money and letters addressed to her poured into the Battle Creek post office. She heard from friends she had not seen in years: George Thompson, Samuel May, Gerrit Smith. Three donations, in particular, astonished her; they came from Ireland, across the sea, and the names of the donors were completely unknown to her.

Despite all this she preferred to think afterward that it was not only love or care or medicine that forced her to get well. It was Abraham Lincoln's Emancipation Proclamation that really pumped the green strength back into her body. When the news flashed over the telegraph wires to Battle Creek on January 1, 1863, Sojourner Truth quite simply could no longer afford to be sick. The President had kept his promise and was indeed freeing all the slaves in the rebel states. She had to get back to work. By the time spring came, she was out and as she put it, "budding with the trees," well enough to leave the Merritt home and return to her own family.

But by that time one less member of Sojourner's family was in Battle Creek. James Caldwell, Hannah's son, had joined the army. Mr. Lincoln had finally given the order to recruit Negro troops; James had signed up with the all-Negro 54th Massachusetts Regiment, and was wearing the uniform of a Union soldier. As she convalesced at home, she would have enjoyed letters from James letting his family know what life was like for a Negro soldier in a crack Negro regiment. But the boy never wrote. Any news she had of the 54th was news that her younger grandson Sammy read aloud from the pages of *The Anti-Slavery Standard*.

One week the paper said the men of James's regiment were refusing to accept their pay from the government, because Congress had ruled that colored troops should be paid less than white.

The white commander of the 54th, Colonel Robert Shaw, had told the Secretary of War that his men would never accept the insult of receiving less pay than other American soldiers.

In June the paper carried a description of the regiment's first public appearance. The troops, said *The Standard,* had marched with beautiful precision through the crooked streets of Boston to drill on the Common. Thousands of people had come out to watch those straight-backed, proud young Negro men marching behind their young colonel and to see the banners flying.

In July there was no news of the 54th, and only bad news elsewhere. The Union armies were making a desperate stand in Pennsylvania. Reinforcements were being rushed from northern cities, but there was much resentment in those cities about the draft. Riots had erupted in the streets of New York, worse riots than Sojourner could ever remember. For four days wild mobs had rushed through the streets, burning houses and killing Negroes.

Why? The paper said the poor white people in New York, most of whom were Irish, were angry about the new Conscription Act. A man with three hundred dollars could pay another man to fight in his place, but the poor had no choice but to march off to war. And New York was full of Copperheads, men who sympathized with the rebel cause. They were always ready to turn the discontent of poor white people into a riot against colored citizens.

Ferries leaving New York, said *The Standard,* sagged to the waterline with refugees. Police stations and arsenals were packed with Negro citizens who were afraid to set foot on the street. Mobs had burned down the Colored Orphan Asylum and hundreds of houses. The bodies of dead Negroes dangled from lampposts. Only after four days of insanity had the city finally grown quiet.

When people at last came to their senses, they looked for a scapegoat. "It was all the fault of the Irish," they said. But *The Standard* published reports of many Irish families who had risked their lives to hide Negro strangers in their homes while the mob howled past, outside.

The New York City regiments who might have defended the city's colored citizens were in Pennsylvania, fighting Lee. Only men too maimed or crippled to be at the front had been left to keep order in the city.

If possible, the news during August was even worse, and this time the bad news came closer to the little house where Sojourner rested. The soldiers of the 54th had fought a battle at Fort Wagner, South Carolina. They had faced a withering fire against im-

"Rioters chasing Negro women and children through the vacant lots on Lexington Avenue" is the caption for this picture that appeared in Harper's Weekly, *August 1, 1863.*

COURTESY NEW YORK HISTORICAL SOCIETY

*A combat correspondent recorded the attack of the 54th Massachusetts
Colored Regiment on Fort Wagner, South Carolina,* Harper's Weekly,
August 8, 1863.

possible odds. According to *The Standard*, the regiment had lost
"every field officer and every captain, and only a lieutenant had
remained to order it to retreat." Colonel Shaw himself had been
seen to fall on the very ramparts of the fort.

The paper continued, "The Charleston papers all say that six
hundred and fifty of our killed were buried on the Sunday morning after the assault. This extraordinary proportion of killed to
wounded could not have been reached without an indiscriminate
murdering of our soldiers after they had fallen wounded and helpless. . . . Unofficial reports say the Negroes have been sold into
slavery and that the white officers are treated with unmeasured
abuse."

And James?

A brown envelope arrived for Sojourner. It was from the War
Department. James Caldwell was reported "missing in action" at

James Island, the day before the battle of Fort Wagner. "He's hidin' somewhere," Sammy insisted. "It wouldn't be easy to kill James." Sojourner prayed that it was so.

She was tired of convalescing. She just had to get out and help. Weren't there Negro soldiers right nearby? She could help care for them. The first Michigan Regiment of Colored Soldiers was stationed only a hundred miles away in Detroit. Maybe she could not do much for James at this time, but she could make sure those boys had a good Thanksgiving.

She went out on the streets, buttonholing passersby, knocking on doors, collecting donations. In the two weeks that she did this, only one man treated her rudely.

"Who are you?" she asked him, surprised.

"The only son of my mother," he snapped.

She looked at him in relief. "I am glad there are no more," she said.

Thanksgiving Day, Sojourner Truth arrived at the gates of Camp Ward, Detroit, in a carriage that creaked and groaned under the weight of roast turkeys, nuts, raisins, fruit cakes, pies, and candies. She was waved past by the sentry; the troops were expecting her. Sojourner had come armed with a new song, one she had made up especially for the First Michigan Regiment. She sent the words of her song flying across the parade ground to the tune of "John Brown's Body," until she had them all singing the verses with her.

We are the valiant soldiers who've 'listed for the war;
We are fighting for the Union, we are fighting for the law;
We can shoot a rebel farther than a white man ever saw,
  As we go marching on . . .

Look there above the center, where the flag is waving bright;
We are going out of slavery, we are bound for freedom's light!
We mean to show Jeff Davis how the Africans can fight,
  As we go marching on . . .

Father Abraham has spoken, and the message has been sent;
The prison doors have opened, and out the prisoners went
To join the sable army of African descent,
  As we go marching on . . .

But very soon the war work that Sojourner found to do around Battle Creek was not enough to keep her busy. She had the feeling there was a more important task waiting for her somewhere.

Ever since the day Lincoln had pronounced his Emancipation Proclamation, Sojourner Truth had had a great longing to meet the first antislavery President. Now it occurred to her she might combine two things: see the President, and perhaps learn from him where she was most needed. She decided to go to Washington.

Her friends were astonished. "It's a long trip to Washington, Sojourner. You might fall sick on the way."

She only shook her head. "I'm taking Sammy along with me, this time. Besides, I'll be stopping in New York to rest and see my friends. It's better I go now before I'm too old to travel and too old to work."

She waited for the snow to melt and the spring sun to dry out the roads. At last, in early June, she packed a good supply of new "shadows" and a stack of homemade songs into a carpet bag. Once again, selling these would pay her way. She carried a small autograph book, too—her *Book of Life*. She liked to have people she admired sign their names there. She wanted to be sure to get the signature of Abraham Lincoln.

Her preparations completed, she and Sammy set out for the East. To her astonishment it was like a home-coming all the way. In New York, her arrival created a sensation. Had not Harriet Beecher Stowe's article in *The Atlantic Monthly*, based on the rumor of Sojourner's death, reported that Sojourner Truth had "passed away from among us as a wave of the sea?" Yet here, in the flesh, was Sojourner!

Mrs. Stowe's article had made Sojourner Truth known to many people who had never heard of her before and who cared not a bean for the antislavery struggle. But these people, like so many others, were interested in celebrities and anxious to hear Sojourner now that they had the chance. She spoke and sang to large audiences in Manhattan and in Williamsburgh, across the East River. In Brooklyn she addressed the congregation of Henry Ward Beecher at Plymouth Church—from the same pulpit where before the war he had so stirred his congregation by auctioning off a tiny, frightened slave girl.

She had so many invitations to speak or to visit old friends, that it seemed for a while as if the old woman and her grandson would never get to Washington. But at last the pair again were on their way.

It was easy enough to get to the city of Washington, but not so easy to get into see President Lincoln. While an old friend was busy pulling strings to get Sojourner an appointment, Sojourner took time to walk around the dirt streets. It was her first visit to any southern town. Never had she seen so many of her own people gathered together in a single place, and never so many people of any color living in such misery.

In addition to the regular Negro population of the city that had lived there before the war, there were twenty thousand freedmen from the South. Long before Lincoln's Proclamation, the contrabands had started filtering in. They were fleeing the rebel armies, headed for Mr. Lincoln's city where folks said they would be safe. The contrabands believed that if they could reach Mr. Lincoln's city, the President would free them. But they found no room, much less real freedom, in that crowded wartime capital.

The city authorities jammed them into rickety barracks and shack towns hastily constructed on marshy ground by the Washington Canal. Houses were sometimes built one on top of the other for lack of ground. The rooms had no light, no air. Rain and snow sifted in through the roof and stinking water oozed up between the floor boards. Entire families were squeezed into rooms that were not more than six by eight feet in size. During the winter, the Freedmen's Relief Association had regularly reported the deaths of tiny children from freezing or pneumonia.

"Five children froze to death last winter in Kendall Green Barracks," Sojourner was told. "When we investigated, we found most families there had neither wood nor coal. Even in winter they have only rags to wear and their bedding is no better."

But it was summer when Sojourner first walked around those hovels. In summer, the mosquitoes and flies took over, and in the heat smallpox spread like a brushfire. Worst of all, the year around there was no work for men who knew only how to plant cotton or to weed corn or tobacco. Sojourner saw able-bodied men sitting around, day after day, waiting for the end of the war so they could go home to farm.

The Emancipation Proclamation had made very little difference in the day-to-day lives of these people. Washington officials now called them freedmen instead of contrabands. Otherwise, nothing had changed.

The sarcastic firm little woman with whom Sojourner was staying spent her spare moments working among the wounded in a hospital. "You'll have no trouble finding work to do in Washington, Sojourner," she said. "We desperately need capable, strong hands."

One bright Saturday morning in October, the doors of the White House at last opened to the traveler from Battle Creek. Sojourner arrived to find a dozen people already waiting. At nine, the President walked in, tall but very stooped. She watched as he took care of his callers. She was thoroughly enjoying her wait. Once a friend had complained to her of Lincoln's slowness in making decisions. She had replied, "Oh, wait, child. Have patience. It takes a great while to turn about this great ship of state." Watching the grooved careworn face now, noticing the gentle courtesy with which he turned to each caller, whether white or colored, she was glad she had defended him on that earlier occasion.

At last it was her turn. "I never heard of you before you were talked of for President," she very soon confided.

He smiled. "Well, I heard of you, years and years before I ever thought of being President. Your name was well known in the Middle West."

Later she told him she believed him to be the best President the country had ever had. But Lincoln would not accept her compliment. He mentioned several other presidents, who, he thought, were at least as good, including George Washington.

Sojourner looked at him quietly, then looked away and shrugged. "They may have been good to others, but they neglected to do anything for my race. Washington had a good name, but his name didn't reach to us."

But Lincoln was insistent. "They would have done just as I have done, if the time had been ripe."

She left without asking the President how she could help win the war. She had not forgotten her reason for coming. But looking around the city during those weeks that she had waited to see him, she had realized she would have no trouble finding a worthwhile task by herself. There was so much to be done right here.

The Freed People

TWENTY SIX

&~ Sojourner returned from her appointment with Lincoln to find an impatient-looking gentleman in a clerical collar waiting for her. Although she had never met him before he smiled at her in recognition, then introduced himself as the Reverend Henry Highland Garnet. Would Sojourner Truth address two meetings at his church to help raise money for the Colored Soldiers' Aid Society? She was glad to. She had recognized the name. For many years Reverend Garnet had been a leader of her people.

The next evening, in the Quaker gown and white Quaker bonnet that she had adopted as her formal dress while living in Battle

Creek, Sojourner stood ready to face the stylishly dressed congregation at Garnet's church. While they waited for the people
to file in, the minister pointed out to her that many of those in the
audience had never been slaves. Even before the war there were
four times as many free Negroes as there were slaves in the District. Slavery and low wages had kept white workers from settling
in Washington, so that for years the city had had to count on free
Negroes to do any skilled work. They were the carpenters, bricklayers, shoemakers, printers, tailors, and cabinetmakers. Some of
the city's best hotels and restaurants had long been run or even
owned by free Negroes. Many had handsome homes and sent
their children to schools they organized themselves.

"The free colored people of Washington have always had to
pay city taxes, like other citizens," Garnet told her, "but the city
would never let our children go to the schools supported by our
taxes. So we started our own schools and paid our own teachers.
We took care of our own poor, too, until the freedmen started
pouring in to the city. There are three times as many colored
people in the city now as there were before the war, and most of
them are in terrible need. We can't possibly take care of all these
ourselves. We're swamped."

The following weeks, Sojourner Truth stood among tents and
makeshift barracks on an island in the middle of the Potomac
River. Shivering in the wind, she addressed a very different audience. In the throng of freedmen facing her there, her eyes picked
out ragged old men with grizzled beards, fathers with small children clinging to their backs, mothers carrying tiny babies bundled
up in old sacks. The tattered clothing of these people was patched
together from whatever the armies had left behind—old tents,
burlap bags, blue and gray blankets. Peering over her spectacles,
Sojourner's sharp eyes noticed more than one makeshift coat
carefully fastened with smooth wooden splinters.

The young white lieutenant escorting her sighed. "Every day, more of these people come straggling in from Virginia. Every last one of them's half-starved when he arrives, but every one of them just has to get to Mr. Lincoln's city. What can we do? We've tried getting them jobs in the North, but the white workers up there don't want it. They're afraid of the competition after the war." He ran his fingers anxiously through his hair. "In any case, not one of the freedmen wants to go north. It's not that they don't want to work, as some would claim. I know what I'm talking about. These people will take any kind of work, if we can only find something for them to do. But they're all afraid to get too far from home. They want to be sure to go back when the war ends."

That day Sojourner looked down into that crowd of ragged people with their hopeful faces raised up to her, and sang again

Another correspondent recorded Negro slaves escaping out of slavery, Harper's Weekly, May 7, 1864.
COURTESY SCHOMBURG COLLECTION, NEW YORK PUBLIC LIBRARY

the song she had composed for the First Michigan Regiment. Here, its words seemed even more appropriate than when she had sung it outside of Detroit.

They will have to pay us wages, the wages of their sin;
They will have to bow their foreheads to their colored kith
  and kin;
They will have to give us house-room, or the roof will tumble
  in,
  As we go marching on . . .

Her voice rose in the chill autumn air, its strange, deep tones soaring over the ragged gathering.

We hear the proclamation, massa, hush it as you will;
The birds will sing it to us, hopping on the cotton hill;
The possum up the gum tree couldn't keep it still,
  As he went climbing on . . .

But even as she sang, she was wondering what she could do to really help her people.

Then she heard that her old friend Josephine Griffing had come to Washington as the local agent of the National Freedmen's Relief Association. Sojourner went immediately to see her. Josephine flushed with delight at the unexpected encounter.

"I know just the place for you, Sojourner," she said. "Freedman's Village. It's a model village established by the army on General Lee's estate in Arlington, and you're exactly the kind of person we've been looking for to instruct the women. Most of them have been field hands all their lives and have everything to learn about keeping house. You could be a great help to them, if you only would!"

Before deciding, Sojourner crossed the Potomac to Arlington Heights to inspect Freedman's Village. The neat little houses laid out in a perfect square were a huge improvement over the miserable shacks and tents she had seen elsewhere around Washington. She liked the frank, firm face of the young superintendent, Captain George Carse.

"We've put some of the freedmen to work up the road, tilling abandoned rebel farms," he said. "They're raising food there for the Union Army." He gestured toward some low buildings. "In these shops we're training other men as blacksmiths, wheelwrights, carpenters, tailors, shoemakers. It's wonderful to see how anxious they all are to learn new skills. But Mrs. Griffing is quite right—we're in desperate need of someone to instruct the women. At present, we have absolutely no one."

Several days later, Sojourner Truth dictated a letter to Amy Post in Rochester:

> *Freedman's Village, Va.,*
> *November 17, 1864*

> *Dear Friend:*
> *I am at Freedman's Village. . . . I think I can be useful and will stay. The people here seem to think a great deal of me and want to learn the way we live in the North. I am listened to with attention and respect, and from all things, I judge it is the will of both God and the people that I should remain. Ask Mr. Oliver Johnson to please send me* The Standard *while I am here, as many of the colored people like to hear what is going on and to know what is being done for them. Sammy, my grandson, reads for them. . . .*

> *Your friend,*
> SOJOURNER TRUTH

Two weeks later, she received her official commission, certifying: "The National Freedmen's Relief Association has appointed Sojourner Truth to be a counselor to the freed people at Arlington Heights, Va."

In the early morning air of Arlington Heights, Sojourner Truth's voice exhorting the women soon became as familiar as the notes of the bugle playing reveille—"Be clean! Be clean! For cleanliness is godliness."

Most of the women with whom she worked had lived only in windowless cabins with dirt floors, eating their meals with their hands from the skillet where the food was cooked. At night, after their work in the fields was over, they had wrapped their bodies in blankets, too tired even to peel off the tow-linen shifts they wore throughout the week.

When a woman worked in the fields "from can to can't," as Sojourner knew, it did not leave much time for keeping a cabin or

Freedmen photographed outside a barracks in Freedman's Village by the famous Civil War photographer, Mathew B. Brady.
REPRODUCED FROM THE COLLECTIONS OF THE LIBRARY OF CONGRESS

small children clean—even had there been anyone to teach her how. But now, at Arlington Village, the eagerness of these women to learn new ways amazed her. It was not long before the bedding could be seen every morning airing in the open, outside the little houses of Freedman's Village. Children were sitting down to eat with freshly scrubbed hands. Brooms were whisking over the bare boards of the cabin floors. Clothing was carefully mended with stitches that were neither too long nor too short, and children's hair was braided into neat pigtails wrapped in strips of bright rag.

Occasionally, when she found time (which was not often), Sojourner would slip into the schoolhouse and sit among the children as they did their lessons. Men and women older than she were there, too, many sitting on the floor, using the benches for desks and doing their lessons along with the children.

"I had intended to take only as many as I could provide with desks," the Yankee teacher told her helplessly, "but every day more children and parents—and even grandparents—slip in, and I cannot bear their disappointment when I turn them away. So I just fit them in as best I can. It is wonderful to see such interest."

Yet even here in Freedman's Village, where they had so many friends, Sojourner found that the ex-slaves were not safe. Sometimes raiding parties of hoodlums from across the Maryland border invaded the neighborhood and kidnapped small Negro children. The mothers were so accustomed to having their children sold away that they did not know how to protect them nor even that it was within their power to do so. Even some of the guards could not be trusted. One mother who had complained to a guard about hoodlum attacks had been slapped into the guardhouse.

"Why didn't you go straight to Captain Carse?" Sojourner asked when she learned this. "Don't you know you are free now? There are laws to protect you and your children. The Marylanders have no right to steal children. You must learn your rights. When you do, you will find that the government will back you up."

After a few more such conversations, the women were convinced. The next Maryland raiding party was greeted by screaming, scratching, biting mothers, prepared to kill to protect their children. The men, in shock, fled back across the river, leaving two shoes and a torn shirt on the road for the women to carry back as trophies.

Shortly after, Sojourner was walking outside the village when a burly youth accosted her. "Old lady," he said grimly. "You had better shut your mouth and mind your own business if you don't want to be locked up."

But he found the "old lady" unintimidated and her cane whipping the air as she leaned her dark face forward to peer into his pale one. "I'll make this United States rock like a cradle, if you so much as attempt such a thing," she hissed. She had no witness to prove it, but she claimed later that that muscular young man scampered up the road like a spanked puppy.

Sojourner was still working among the women at Freedman's Village when Lee surrendered to Grant at Appomattox Courthouse. Six days later, the terrible news came to Freedman's Village, as it came to all the nation: Abraham Lincoln was dead.

Above the door of every house around the square, black rags flapped in the light April breeze. But as Sojourner walked among the sorrowing people, she found the freedmen wept not only for grief. Who would protect them now that Mr. Lincoln was gone? Already it was rumored that they would be sent back into slavery. She reassured them, "You are all free now. Your masters can't hurt you or take you back." But it was not easy to convince people who had spent their lives in slavery.

Many of the freedmen had never seen the President. Now they felt they must see him before he was buried. A group of men from Freedman's Village marched all the way to the White House to stand barefoot in the seemingly endless line that wound past the silver-studded casket in the East Room. That day there was no guard to check the invitations at the door: black and white were equally welcome to call. And all day they came, both black and white, for their look at Mr. Lincoln—and to say good-bye.

It was fall when Sojourner was asked by the Bureau of Refugees, Freedmen, and Abandoned Lands to leave Freedman's Village. She was needed even more urgently to help the surgeon in charge of Freedman's Hospital "to promote order, cleanliness, industry, and virtue among the patients."

Freedman's Hospital, like other army hospitals, was jammed with war wounded, and the soldiers suffered terribly from lack of attention. There were not enough doctors and the few nurses were, for the most part, too inexperienced to be much help.

Now Sojourner's deep voice, exhorting, "Be clean, be clean!" was heard ringing up and down the hospital wards, just as it had up the lanes of Freedman's Village. She instructed the nurses, showing them how to make beds and to wash infected wounds and bodies covered with bed sores and lice, and how to change bandages fastened like tree bark to wounds by dried blood. And on Sundays, she always managed somehow to find time also to preach to the men and to sing them the old hymns she had learned during her long travels and the songs she had made up herself.

It was during those months at Freedman's Hospital that Sojourner, for the first time in her life, found herself dependent on streetcars.

When she had first come to Washington, each streetcar route

had had its Jim Crow car. But Lincoln had signed a law outlawing this discrimination in Washington's public transportation.
Now there was no Jim Crow car; but the street railroad employed
the same conductors as before, and none of them would stop to
take on a Negro passenger when he could avoid it. Instead of
riding in a Jim Crow car, Sojourner and other Negro people now
often did not get to ride at all.

One day, starting back to the hospital, Sojourner was determined to ride. Her load was particularly heavy, her bag filled with
chewing tobacco, candy, and several books for a former field
hand who had learned to read while in the army. Already she had
signaled several cars with her umbrella, but the conductors managed to look right through her. Suddenly, passersby were startled
by three tremendous yells—"I want to ride! I want to ride! *I
want to ride!*"

The cries split the air like an Indian war whoop. Horses reared
in panic. Coachmen slammed on their brakes. Passersby turned
in their tracks. From the street, noses could be seen pressed flat as
pennies against the panes of closed windows.

The traffic had blocked the track, and before the streetcar
could free itself to start again, Sojourner had leaped aboard,
umbrella and all. Her gray skirts flapped around her long limbs
like a Union Jack whipping around a flag pole. The crowd roared
with glee. "Ha, ha, ha. The old woman has beaten him."

The infuriated conductor ordered Sojourner to stand on the
front platform behind the horses. "I'll put you off, if you don't do
as I say," he bellowed.

Ignoring his threats, she seated herself peacefully on a bench.
"I am a passenger and shall sit with the other passengers," she
said with her usual dignity.

He moved his arm as if to strike her. Her eyes flashed.

"I am not a Marylander or a Virginian to tremble at your

bullying," she cried. "I am from the Empire State of New York and know the laws as well as you."

On her next visit to town, she found herself having to chase a car up the track until it was forced to stop to take on white passengers. "Shame on you to make a lady run so!" she panted, as she clambered aboard.

This conductor, too, would have thrown her off, but a gentleman in the uniform of a Union general angrily forbade it. "The old woman has as much right to ride as any of us. Let her be," he ordered.

The "shadows" sold by Sojourner to pay her way were really postcards. This one was copyrighted by her in 1864.

COURTESY SCHOMBURG
COLLECTION, NEW YORK
PUBLIC LIBRARY

Three weeks later, Sojourner Truth was escorting a new nurse to the hospital. The two of them had taken seats in an empty car at the beginning of the streetcar route when two white ladies sat down directly opposite them and began to whisper so loudly, pursing their mouths and casting disapproving glances across the aisle, that the new nurse's head soon was drooping almost to her knees with embarrassment. She had never before ridden a streetcar, never sat on a level with white folks, and certainly never wished to do so again.

But Sojourner was not in the least intimidated. She stared right back at the two white women until they lowered their eyes. At last one of them nervously cleared her throat and in a weak, refined voice asked the conductor, "Conductor. Oh, conductor, are Negroes supposed to ride these cars?"

Since the conductor seemed uncertain, the woman continued peevishly, "It's a shame and a disgrace. You really ought to have another car for these people."

Sojourner continued to stare. At last she said, "Of course colored people ride the cars. Streetcars are for poor folk, white and colored. Carriages are for grand ladies and gentlemen." She pointed sweetly out the window. "See! There are some nice empty carriages, just waiting to take you three or four miles for six cents. Is that too much for you to pay?"

A rosy flush spread over the cheeks of both white ladies. Within seconds they had swooped out of the streetcar and into a carriage.

But Sojourner's battle with the street railways was not over. The final round came one day when she was shopping with her white friend, Laura Haviland. Her friend was exhausted, but she knew she would probably not be allowed to ride accompanied by Sojourner, and she was not willing to ride without her. Together they agreed on a strategy. Sojourner stepped aside while Laura Haviland signaled the car. As soon as it stopped, both women jumped on. But the conductor gave the tall old Negro woman a furious shove. "Get out of the way and let this lady in," he said.

"I am a lady, too," said Sojourner, and sat down.

However, in order to reach the hospital they had to change cars. The next conductor grabbed Sojourner by one shoulder, jerked her around and ordered her off. Sojourner's friend angrily protested.

"Does she belong to you?" asked the conductor.

"She belongs to humanity," replied Laura Haviland.

"Then let humanity take her and go," he barked and slammed Sojourner against the door.

Her shoulder ached so, she could hardly move her arm. When the doctors at Freedmen's Hospital examined it, they found it had been pushed out of joint. The Freedmen's Bureau promptly offered her a lawyer, and she sued the street railway for assault and battery. A week later, the conductor who had abused her was out of a job.

Sojourner said later, "Before the trial was ended, the inside of those cars looked like pepper and salt. A few weeks later, Mrs. Haviland saw some colored women looking wistfully toward a car. Without their doing more than that, the conductor stops and says, pleasant as you please, 'Walk in, ladies.' "

Forty Acres

TWENTY SEVEN

&> But as the months after Lincoln's death stretched into a year, and more than a year, Sojourner was becoming obsessed with one question: what would happen to all these jobless people, waiting in such misery in the shadow of the capitol dome? Someone, she felt, had to find a plan.

Sometimes she helped Josephine Griffing by distributing used clothing in a church basement for the Freedmen's Relief Association. She would scold the ragged women for their pushing and shoving while she handed out dresses, trousers, shirts, jackets, and shoes as fast as she could check them for size. But she was

ashamed of her own scolding. These women had such good reason for impatience. Many had left little children all alone in their
icy shacks while they tried to get clothing to cover them. Others
had borrowed their neighbor's only gown to come for a dress of
their own.

Josephine Griffing went north in a desperate attempt to get
more help. As the Washington agent of the National Freedmen's
Relief Association, she addressed large audiences in northern
cities, pleading for food, clothing, bedding, lumber, nails, window
panes, and money. Despite the soup kitchens set up by the Freedmen's Bureau, many of the freed slaves in the national capital
were actually starving. Many northerners asked, "Why doesn't the
Freedmen's Bureau do more for the freedmen? Isn't that what
it's there for? Let it teach them trades and find them jobs."

Others said, "The government's already done too much. Our
mistake was in freeing the slaves. They'll only work when they are
forced."

The Freedmen's Bureau had been set up to educate the freed
slaves and to protect their new rights. It was doing its best. But
the Bureau and its chief, General Oliver Otis Howard, had powerful political enemies and could never get enough money from
Congress. Those northerners who had been most reluctant to fight
the war in the first place, now fought every attempt to help the
men that war had freed. Meanwhile, the freedmen were nursing
a new and stubborn dream.

In January 1865, when General Sherman was pursuing the
remnants of the Confederate Army northward, he had issued,
with the acquiescence of the War Department, his Special Field
Orders No. 15. The General authorized the freedmen to take
possession of the land on the Sea Islands, off the coast between
Charleston, South Carolina, and Jacksonville, Florida, and of
the abandoned rice plantations for thirty miles inland. Each man
was to have forty acres and a mule for the duration of the war,

with the understanding that the land would then be given to him permanently by Congress. The faith of the government, according to the military inspector in that region, was "solemnly pledged to maintain them in possession."

The news of this land division and of the government's promise had spread far beyond the Sea Islands. Among the freedmen in Washington and the camps beyond, it was common gossip that, "come the end of the war," the government would give each man land and an animal to pull his plow.

It seemed a brave and sensible idea to Sojourner. She remembered very well how Gerrit Smith had given land to the freedmen up in North Elba, after New York State had freed its slaves. How else could newly freed slaves live? Now, wherever she went that winter of 1865–66 in Washington, she heard the old rumor repeated: "Just wait, wait a little longer. Government'll give every colored man forty acres and a mule. Soon now! Just wait and see."

At first, the rumor had been that the gift would come from Lincoln. Then Lincoln had died, and the sorrow and the fear of being returned to their masters had swept through the freedmen's camps. But when the fear did not materialize, the dream of land returned.

For a while the men in the shacks along the Washington Canal had spoken about having the land by Christmas. But Christmas came, a cold Christmas with the wind cutting through the walls of the ramshackle huts, and still no gift from the government. Yet the rumor of land would not die. Now the freedmen said the land would be distributed on New Year's Day.

It snowed on New Year's. The snow drifted through the sagging roofs and gaping paneless windows. Sojourner passed a long line of shivering freedmen standing outside a soup house. Thin soup and bread were the only causes of celebration that day.

But a fresh rumor began to grow—and this one proved all too

true. President Andrew Johnson was returning to their former owners all abandoned lands, as well as the land confiscated by the army. There would be no land to distribute to ex-slaves.

At the same time, many southern states were passing new laws, called Black Codes, that would restrict the freedman almost as much as if he were still a slave. A freed slave now risked his very life by returning home. One man had returned to claim his wife and children and was shot dead by his former master for having had the audacity to leave in the first place. Others tilled the fields but could collect no pay. And the Union Army was being withdrawn from southern forts. In the South there was no longer any official protection for the black man who dared insist on his rights.

While Sojourner Truth and Josephine Griffing and Laura Haviland handed out old clothing and worried about children growing up with too little food and no schooling, and men sitting around without jobs—the politicians seesawed back and forth.

By the close of 1866, Congress was once again in the control of men called Radical Republicans who opposed Johnson's policies. Over the President's veto, the new Congress passed the first of four bills called Reconstruction Acts. The first bill sent the army back into the South. It gave freedmen the vote and disqualified ex-Confederate leaders. The Black Codes were outlawed. New state constitutions were to be drawn up by delegates elected by all the eligible voters in a state.

But there was not a word in that bill about land.

Sojourner decided she could not stay in Washington any longer. She could not bear to see men rotting, jobless, their families hungry, and no solution. If no one else would, she decided, she herself would have to find these men jobs.

In the winter of 1867, the old woman headed into western New York, still escorted by her grandson Sammy. She knew that many towns, like Rochester, had lost young men in the war and needed workers to replace them. Surely, in those towns, there would be jobs for freed slaves.

For several months, Sojourner Truth traveled around, with her cane and her white Quaker bonnet, addressing meetings. As she

"The First Vote" was the title of this woodcut from Harper's Weekly, *November 16, 1867.*

COURTESY NEW YORK HISTORICAL SOCIETY

had expected, she found many jobs available, and returned to Washington to find the men to fill them. It was not hard to find men. Hundreds were willing to move north now if it meant work. But a few jobs was no solution. Washington alone had twenty thousand freedmen, and many others waited in the refugee camps of the southern states. Years earlier, in speaking of the Underground Railroad as a means of freeing slaves, Frederick Douglass had said that it was "like bailing out the ocean with a teaspoon." Sojourner felt that might be said, too, of her attempt to find employment for the freedmen.

But even worse, she began to realize that sending young men north left many children and old people alone to shift for themselves. The situation grew not better but worse.

The children especially worried her. Their thin shadows darted in and out of the muddy Washington alleys, their large eyes opening wide as shutters at the deep voice coming from this tall old woman. She had stood and watched boys of nine and ten hauled off to jail. Next week they would be back on the street, she knew. And the week after that, back in jail.

People complained when the government spent money on schools or training for the freedmen. But she was beginning to wonder why the people did not protest the money that was spent on supporting jails and the police. Was that a better use of the taxpayer's money?

It was now quite apparent that Congress would never give land to the freedmen in the southern states. But at the same time, Congress seemed perfectly willing to give away land in other parts of the country. Men who wanted to build railroads were receiving millions of acres in the West. Entire mountains were being deeded to other men who wanted to mine land for ore. Indian tribes were being given vast reservations in exchange for their promise to settle down and keep the peace.

Gradually, as Sojourner mulled over these facts, a new plan took shape in her mind. Why shouldn't the government also give the freedmen land in the West? There were still millions of acres of wide-open uninhabited land.

It cost the nation money to keep these Negroes barely alive, to jail children, to keep sickness from spreading. And the nation did not profit from money spent that way. The same money could be spent in resettling the freedmen in the West. Give them land, homes, tools, farm animals. Then the whole nation would benefit.

A year or so earlier, a famous editor, Theodore Tilton, had asked to write the story of Sojourner's life. On that occasion, she is said to have replied, "I am not ready to be writ up yet, for I have still lots to accomplish."

Now, at seventy-three years of age, Sojourner Truth set out to prove this by embarking on the last great mission of her life.

Give Them Land

TWENTY EIGHT

𝕰 Sojourner Truth expected the government to welcome her new plan. To give the freedmen land in the West made good sense to her, and she thought it would appeal to the taxpayers. She went first to see General Howard, the chief of the Freedmen's Bureau, and explained her idea to him. He listened intently, nodding his black-bearded head at each of her arguments.

"It is certainly an interesting idea, Sojourner," he agreed. "But unfortunately, only Congress has the power to give away federal land. I'm afraid I can't be of much help. The Freedmen's Bureau is barely able to keep alive these days. We get few favors from

Congress. Why don't you drop in on Charles Sumner? He might be the one to help you."

Her cane clacking on the flagstone sidewalk, Sojourner Truth marched over to see the Senator from Massachusetts. Sumner was an antislavery man. He had defeated Daniel Webster almost twenty years earlier, when the voters of Massachusetts had gagged at Webster's vote for the Fugitive Slave Bill. Only a few years ago, Sumner had introduced a bill in the Senate to give the ex-slaves land in the South. The bill, of course, had been defeated; but Sojourner hoped she could count on Sumner's help now.

The Senator unfortunately that day was in a great hurry to get to an appointment, and glanced repeatedly at his watch as Sojourner explained her plan. At last he said, "Congress will only do what people force it to do, Sojourner. It's the people you must convince. If they put pressure on Congress to give western land to the freedmen, Congress will do it. Of that you may be sure. But somehow you've got to reach the people."

She realized that he was right; there was no other way. If the ex-slaves were ever to get land, someone would have to stir up the people, force them to see, and make them speak up. What was more, it was equally clear that Sojourner Truth herself would have to do the stirring. There was no one else to do it. When she realized that, the next step was simple. She left Washington and headed north.

There were no riots in the streets of Providence, Rhode Island, the day she opened her campaign to give land to the ex-slaves—no riots such as there had been on that brisk February day twenty years earlier, when she and George Thompson had started their tour in nearby Springfield. It was 1870 now, and Sojourner Truth was standing on a platform, holding a petition she had drawn up herself.

A crowd had gathered, today, not to hurl stones or insults, as on that earlier occasion, but to hear a celebrated woman, a famous ex-slave. Times had indeed changed. But the work begun by Garrison, Pillsbury, and all the other antislavery men and women with whom she had worked in more dangerous times was only half-completed. America still had a debt to pay the slaves it had freed. Sojourner Truth stood here today without those friends of long ago, to tell the people how that debt might be paid.

Her petition said:

TO THE SENATE AND HOUSE OF REPRESENTATIVES,
In Congress Assembled:

Whereas, From the faithful and earnest representations of Sojourner Truth (who has personally investigated the matter) we believe that the freed colored people in and about Washington, dependent upon government for support, would be greatly benefited and might become useful citizens by being placed in a position to support themselves;

We, the undersigned, therefore earnestly request your honorable body to set apart for them a portion of the public land in the West, and erect buildings thereon for the aged and infirm, and otherwise legislate so as to secure the desired results.

Sitting on the platform, in her sober dark gown with the fringed white wool shawl and chaste Quaker bonnet, holding her petition in her hand, she looked like a sad old grandmother. A circlet of graying hair peeked out beneath the bonnet and her great black eyes behind the gold-rimmed spectacles were mournful. But as she stood up to speak, her gaunt and bony six-foot frame was erect. One gnarled hand gripped the head of her cane, the other waved her petitions aloft. Her eyes glowed with anger and her great voice could still penetrate to the farthest seats of a hall. Standing there on the platform, she was like some mighty messenger of her Lord, calling America to account for more than two hundred years of its sins against her people. The truths she spoke came more bluntly from her lips now, as if she realized she had less time in which to speak them.

That day she described to her audience the way the freedmen lived in Washington. And she told how she had so often looked around her at the great public buildings that made the capital city of our country so beautiful. And then she had looked at her people starving in the very shade of those buildings. And she had asked, "Didn't we help pay for all this? We grew the cotton that built the mill towns of your northern cities and gave your people jobs. And where did the money to run your government come from, if not from the people of those towns and the cotton workers of the South? Surely, this great country owes the man who worked in the fields to grow the cotton some return.

"But all the government does for the freedmen in Washington is hand out loaves of bread. That helps no one. It only wastes your money and wastes the men who could be helping build this nation.

"That's why I'm here, today. I've come to explain the situation so you can understand and help change it."

They filled out all her petitions that day. She thought she might already have enough names to impress Congress. A few more such meetings, and Sojourner Truth and Sammy headed back to Washington.

This time, she received a warmer reception in Washington. Fifteen senators took time out to confer with her in the marble room of the Senate Chamber, while the Freedmen's Bureau suddenly decided to settle an old debt and pay her, at last, for the months she had spent working at Freedman's Village and at the hospital. Fifteen dollars a month for twenty-six months of work came to three hundred and ninety dollars.

She sent every penny to Charles Merritt in Battle Creek. She had bought a new house from him, and Sammy's mother, Elizabeth, was already living there with her husband and younger son. Sojourner had to pay off the mortgage.

But except for the back pay and the flattering acclaim, there was no help offered Sojourner Truth in Washington. The senators all said she would need many thousands of names if she really hoped to influence Congress.

So once more the old woman and her grandson turned north, stopping everywhere now to speak and collect signatures, selling "shadows" to help pay their way. Her audiences grew steadily in size. "Go," newspapers now advised their readers. "It may well be the last time we shall see the old lady among us."

But this was not the reason Sojourner wanted people to come. She wanted her audience to get to work and help her collect names. She wanted to send "tons of paper down to Washington for those spouters to chaw on." She spoke at woman's rights meetings, lamenting the fact that women did not yet have the vote. For, she said, she was certain the women would all bring pressure on Congress to support her project—if only they had the political power to do so.

She tried to reach the men through their pocketbooks. Your taxes are being wasted, she told them. Send the freedmen west. Out there, for the same money, you can make good citizens and independent people out of them and they will enrich the country and you with it.

She spoke four times in Philadelphia. On May 4, she was in New York City. In Fall River, she filled three halls. She spoke in

Pawtucket. In Boston, she appeared at a Woman's Rights Convention. On New Year's Day, she addressed an enormous audience assembled at Boston's Tremont Temple to celebrate the Eighth Anniversary of the Emancipation Proclamation.

Time after time, she repeated, "They are living on the government. And there are people taking care of them costing you so much—and it doesn't benefit them at all. It just degrades them worse and worse.

"Take these people," she begged. "Put them in the West where you can enrich them. How much better it will be to give them land. They've earned the right to land for a home, and it would benefit everybody."

Sometimes, she grew angry. "They say, 'Let 'em take care of themselves.' Why, you've taken all that away from them! They ain't got nothin' left. Get these colored people out of Washington,

An 1869 Currier and Ives print, entitled "The Age of Iron," illustrates the average man's opinion of the Woman's Rights movement. Lacking a vote, women could do little to help get land for the freedmen.
COURTESY NEW YORK HISTORICAL SOCIETY

off the government. Put them where they can feed themselves. And soon they will be a people among you.

"I speak these things," she always concluded, "so that when you have a paper come for you to sign, you can sign it."

Sammy or other friends would then go through the audience collecting signatures.

Almost always now, she needed Sammy's arm to guide her off the stage after she made her speech. And afterward, she was often very tired.

They Cannot Get Up

TWENTY NINE

ॐ Early in 1871, Sojourner was at Sam Hill's house in Northampton, Massachusetts, resting up from her campaign, when she
was surprised to receive a letter from Kansas.

Topeka, Kansas, Dec. 31, 1870
SOJOURNER TRUTH—Dear Madam:
I know so much of you by reputation and venerate and love
so much your character that I am induced to write this. I say
I know so much of you, which is true, but it is only by report,
as I have never had the pleasure of meeting you yet. My

object in writing this is to ask and earnestly request that you
make our town a visit. I would very much like to have you
come to my house and make it your home as long as you can
be contented. If you will say you will come, I will send you
the price of your railroad fare and enough to pay additional ex-
penses. Please let me hear from you, and, if possible, convey
the good intelligence that you will come and see us.

Yours very respectfully,
Byron M. Smith

Who was Byron M. Smith? And why would she be receiving an invitation to visit John Brown's state from a stranger? Could it be that the Lord was designating Kansas as the state where the freedmen would settle and appointing her to go and prepare the way?

She had been depressed by the lack of interest shown in her campaign. But this sign of interest seemed to restore her will to work.

She dictated a letter to the editor of the New York *Tribune*, Horace Greeley, enclosing Smith's letter and outlining her project: "I have been crying out in the East, and now an answer comes to me from the West. . . . I made up my mind, last winter, when I saw able men and women taking dry bread from the government to keep from starving that I would devote myself to the cause of getting land for these people where they can work and earn their own living in the West, where the land is so plenty. . . . Everybody says this is a good work. But nobody helps! How glad I will be if you will take hold and give the work a good lift. Please help me with these petitions."

Slowly she turned her steps west—toward Kansas—stopping wherever she could to rouse the people. She spoke for a second time in Providence. It was a year since she had opened her campaign there. Her words now were more impatient. "With all your opportunities for reading and writing, you don't take hold and do anything. My God, I wonder what you are in the world for!"

In Springfield, the same paper that had whipped up the mob against George Thompson, years earlier, now gossiped about Sojourner Truth as if she were one of its favorite citizens, "She is now on her way to a friend of hers and her cause in Kansas and, at her age, she never expects to return."

She was retracing the route she had traveled with Thompson and Samuel May. And now, wherever she went, she was saying good-bye to old friends. In March she spoke in Syracuse, at the same hall in which members of an audience had rushed forward, twenty years earlier, with offers of jobs for five fugitive slaves. Again she visited Gerrit Smith in Peterboro, New York. A letter in Sammy's handwriting had preceded her, "I would like to come out to Peterboro and have a meeting there and see you once more before I go out West as I may never come this way again. Please to send me an answer by return mail. My grandson is with me."

Again she stopped in Rochester, where she stayed with Amy and Isaac Post, and again she trod the hard boards of the platform at Corinthian Hall. Her exasperation was growing. "You ask me what to do for them? Do you want a poor old creature who don't know how to read to tell educated people what to do? I give you the hint, and you ought to know what to do." She seemed to relent a little. "But if you don't know, I can tell you." Patiently, then, as she had at every meeting along her way, she argued her plan.

"The government has given land to the railroads in the West. Can't it do as much for the freedmen? Give them land and something to start with, and have teachers learn them how to read. Then they can be somebody.

"Yes," she told her audience, "that's what I want. And you owe it to them. Because you took away from them all they earned and made them what they are."

She had so little time left and so much to accomplish.

"You take no interest in the colored people," she scolded. "You are the cause of the misery of these poor creatures. For you are the children of those who enslaved them."

That day, speaking in Corinthian Hall, she noticed many empty seats. Yet only the week before, her friends told her, it had been filled to the rafters for a lecture on Joan of Arc. The very thought made her scold her listeners again. "I wish this hall was full to hear me. If someone comes here to talk about a woman you know nothing about and no one knows whether there was such a woman or not, you fill this place. You just want to hear nonsense. I come to tell you something you ought to listen to. But you are ready to help the heathen in foreign lands and don't care for the heathen right about you."

She held out her arms, pleading with those white faces staring up at her. "The blacks can never be much in the South. They cannot get up. As long as the whites have the reins in their hands, how can the colored people get up?"

She knew and her audience knew that hooded men were riding in the South, leaving behind them homes burned to the ground and the dead bodies of black men who had been bold enough to vote.

Sojourner thrust her petitions at her audience. "I want you to sign these to send to Washington. Congress says it will do what the people want. The majority rules. If they want anything good, the people get it. And if they want anything not so good, they get that, too. Now you just send these petitions. And those men in Congress will have something to spout about. I been to hear them," she snorted. "Could make nothing out of what they say.

Send a good man with the petitions, one that will not turn the other side out when he gets to Washington."

An old friend, Methodist bishop Gilbert Haven, originally had offered to help her present her petitions to Congress when she had them ready. But now his church had shifted him from Boston to a post in Atlanta. He had his hands full fighting for the rights of the freedmen in his new diocese. She would have to find someone else to present her petitions in Washington.

Standing now in Corinthian Hall, she repeated, "Let the freedmen be emptied out into the West. Give them land and something to start on. Teach them to read. Then they will *be* somebody. That's all I want to say." She was grateful to be able to sit down again.

One night, not long after, she was walking alone toward Amy Post's home, leaning heavily on her cane. It was late; the lights in the houses she passed were already out. Only occasional pools of light, cast on the street by gas lamps, remained to show her the way. The stars glittered above, in a moonless sky. Just as Ma-Ma used to do so long ago, Sojourner Truth thought now of those stars shining on her large family. But the family of Sojourner Truth was bigger than Ma-Ma and Bomefree could ever have dreamed. It included so many of her people, waiting in shacktowns and crowded barracks, still waiting for land.

"Hey, there, old woman! What are you doing out so late? What's your name?"

Her eyes left the stars and turned back to earth, back to the narrow, poorly lighted street of Rochester. A short man in a policeman's uniform blocked her way. She towered over this puny officer of the law. "I AM THAT I AM," she thundered, whacking her cane on the road. He stepped back startled, as she walked slowly on.

She held two more meetings in Rochester, still asking support for her petitions, before boarding the steamer to Detroit. In Michigan a surprise awaited her. While Sojourner had been working in Washington, Michigan had granted women the right to vote in state elections. Only one thing, as Sojourner well knew, could be responsible for this grand event. The women had been "stirring up the people." Just to think of such success gave her fresh strength for her own work, and she pushed on again in high spirits. At last, in September, Sojourner and Sammy reached Kansas.

They stayed a few days at the home of Byron Smith in Topeka. But she had little time to visit and discuss religion with this friendly stranger. She told him of her dream of land for the freed slaves and of his letter that had seemed to her a sign from the Lord, turning her feet to Kansas in that search. And then she moved on.

North Topeka, Lawrence, Wyandotte, Leavenworth. . . . It was not like the old days in Ohio, when she had driven through the country with a banner and a borrowed horse and buggy, her face shielded from the sun by an old bonnet. Now friends found her halls to speak in, competed for the honor of having her as their guest, and drove her in comfort to the next town in their private carriages.

Wherever she passed, her keen eyes scrutinized the land. This state did indeed seem a good place for her people to settle. Vast acres still waited to be claimed. The land was fertile, the citizens friendly. Yes, she thought Kansas would serve her purpose very well. But she still had to persuade Congress. She needed more signatures.

In February, she was in Iowa, talking to the people. In April, Illinois; Missouri in July. At last, in August, Sojourner and Sammy turned back to Battle Creek. But not to rest. It was a detour. She had decided she was needed there, temporarily, to campaign for Grant's re-election. Moreover, she planned to vote for Grant. After all, had not Michigan given the vote to women?

Sojourner went to register. "Can you read and write?" the registrar wanted to know. She was outraged. What difference did it make?

"I tell you I can't read a book," she told the registrar firmly, "but I can read the people." Was that not far more important for a voter? The registrar did not seem to think so.

"It is Sojourner's determination," reported the Battle Creek paper, "to continue the assertion of her right until she gains it."

Meanwhile, the old woman in the Quaker dress continued to travel through the Middle West—"making majorities" to force Congress to give her people land. At last it seemed she surely must have enough signatures. Now she would return to Washington and present them herself.

Sometime during the long hot summer of 1874, Sojourner returned to Washington with Sammy. Sammy escorted his grandmother as she knocked on Congressional doors.

Sojourner needed a senator who would present her petition officially to Congress. She knocked on the door of one senator after another, remembering as she did so a line in a letter she had received from General Howard a few months earlier. "Many think no more should be done by the general government for the classes rendered helpless by the war and by slavery," he had written.

The Freedmen's Bureau was no longer in existence. Two years earlier, Congress had cut off its money. That same year, an amnesty bill had been passed, restoring the right to vote to all former Confederate leaders. Even Charles Sumner thought the time had come to forgive and forget the bitterness of the war. But Sumner had felt the amnesty bill, if passed by itself, would be a mistake.

He had worked hard to combine it with a second bill which would have outlawed any kind of discrimination against any Negro in any state of the Union.

In his clipped Boston accent, Sumner had argued long hours on the Senate floor. A return to full citizenship for those who fought against the Union is a noble measure, he had said. But would it not also be a noble measure—and a remarkably appropriate one at this time—to make certain of an equally full citizenship for those who were freed by a war in which so many brave men lost their lives?

His arguments were unsuccessful. Only the bill restoring the vote to Confederate leaders was passed. Congress not only refused to guarantee the civil rights of the freedmen; it proceeded instead to deprive many of them of rights they had already won. The Fifteenth Amendment to the Constitution had guaranteed every man the right to vote. Now Congress passed a law disenfranchising the entire population of the District of Columbia. It did not want to risk the possibility that the government of the nation's capital might pass into the hands of Negroes, who by now made up more than twenty-five percent of the city's people.

By the time Sojourner Truth arrived in Washington with Sammy, her petitions tied together with yellow string, even Sumner's door was closed. Sumner had died in March.

But now something so serious and so personal happened that she could not stay to look for another senator to help her present her petitions. Sammy was sick.

At first, Sojourner thought, it was because of the heat. That summer the thick dust drifted up from the sidewalks and sun-baked Washington streets, while the motionless air rested like a rock on the chest. The nights left both of them gasping for breath. She knew Sammy would be more comfortable in the clear-pine-scented air of southern Michigan. Sojourner decided to take him home. They started back, the petitions still tied together with string. It was an old woman helping a young man now, her "reading eyes," as she had always liked to call him.

She got him home, but the Michigan air proved not enough to save her Sammy, who grew steadily worse. In February, Sammy Banks died.

Sojourner, too, fell terribly sick. Paralysis set in on one side of her body. Her eye was half-closed with it and a painful ulcer developed along her leg.

Once again there were rumors of the death of Sojourner Truth. Once again she found herself without money. And once again friends rallied to her aid. It was at this time that a Battle Creek admirer, Frances Titus, brought *Narrative of Sojourner Truth* up to date. To the story that Olive Gilbert had taken down, many years earlier, Mrs. Titus added the news clippings, reminiscences, and letters accumulated during Sojourner's busy public years, as well as many pages of autographs from the book that Sojourner carried everywhere and which she called her *Book of Life*.

Sojourner Truth recovered from her illness. Her friends pronounced it a miracle. But Sojourner was quietly satisfied as to the reason for her recovery. "My good Master kept me," she explained, "for he had something for me to do."

She still had to lay her petitions before Congress.

A Great Glory

THIRTY

৯০ Sojourner Truth never returned to Washington. The petitions rested on the shelf in her new house on College Street—yellow-ing, gathering dust, at last forgotten. It was no use presenting them to Congress now. With every passing year, the country only turned its back more emphatically on the slaves it had set free.

The year after Sammy's death, Rutherford B. Hayes was elected President. Like Lincoln and Grant, the new President was a Republican. But there no longer seemed to be much difference between the Democrats and the Republicans. Men of both parties were primarily concerned with making money—building factories, laying railroad track, digging for copper. There was little concern for the rights of freedmen.

The election had been very close. People whispered that, in order to be allowed to take office, Hayes had made a deal with the southern Democrats. Why, otherwise, did he withdraw the last federal troops from the South, only two months after entering the White House?

Many white southerners had deeply resented having northern troops stationed in the South. But even many of these people recognized that it was only the presence of federal troops that could protect the rights guaranteed to the freedmen by the Fourteenth and Fifteenth Amendments to the Constitution.

The Fourteenth Amendment promised, "No state shall make or enforce any law which shall abridge the privileges or immunities of citizens of the United States; nor shall any State deprive any person of life, liberty or property, without due process of law; nor deny to any person within its jurisdiction the equal protection of the laws."

The Fifteenth Amendment said, "The rights of citizens of the United States to vote shall not be denied or abridged by the United States, or by any State, on account of race, color or previous condition of servitude."

Even with the presence of federal soldiers in the South, these rights were frequently violated. And now Congress intended to leave the freedmen without any protection. To expect such a Congress to have any interest in her petitions, Sojourner felt, would be foolish. Instead of returning to Washington, she turned to other tasks.

Sojourner was now eighty years old. Friends who had watched in astonishment her recovery from her last serious illness, now watched her with even more surprise. Sojourner Truth seemed to be growing younger. Her paralysis completely disappeared. Her hair, which had for many years peeked out in a gray fringe from under the edge of the white Quaker bonnet, was now growing in black. She no longer needed to wear her spectacles. As she put it, "God is putting new glass in the windows of my soul." She fully expected him to send her new teeth, too.

As she had for so many years, she continued to travel and to speak for women's rights. She also spoke up for prison reform, for temperance, and for the rights of working men. Wearing a bright red shawl, she gave the Michigan State Senate her views on capital punishment. "The person who wants to see his fellow beings hung by the neck until dead has a murderous spot in his heart," she said. She could still stand straight as a Catskill hemlock and her deep, resonant voice had lost none of its power to startle and hold an audience.

In the eighty-first year of her life, Sojourner addressed audiences in thirty-six different towns in Michigan. That July in 1878, she was one of three Michigan delegates to the thirtieth anniversary meeting of the first Woman's Rights Convention in Rochester, New York. There she saw her old friend Lucretia Mott for the last time. "Why, Sojourner," said Lucretia in surprise, "how is it that I am so wrinkled and your face is as smooth as can be?"

"Well," said Sojourner, "I have two skins. I have a white skin under and a black one to cover it."

It was about this time that Sojourner and others began to hear an astonishing report. In December of 1877 a movement had started in the southern states, and grown steadily throughout 1878 and 1879. A great migration of freedmen was leaving the South and heading north toward Kansas.

It was only a trickle at first, a few adventurous families and single men leaving the South. But more and more followed. The freedmen had clearly stopped waiting for an indifferent Congress to protect their rights. They were taking matters into their own hands.

The move toward Kansas, however, had not started among those crowded shanties near the Washington Canal whose people Sojourner had worried about for so long, but deep in the lower Mississippi Valley, farther south than the roads of her life had ever taken her. There, during the years of the Reconstruction governments and the Freedmen's Bureau, black men had had a chance to become, for the first time, free and independent citizens. Now, with the army gone, the Freedmen's Bureau gone, the Reconstruction governments fallen—these men saw their independence under attack from all sides. They were not waiting any longer; they were leaving the South on their own.

First, along the trails flanking the Mississippi Valley, had come the roll of wagon wheels, the slow clop-clop of hundreds of patient oxen, the clatter of tools and pots and pans. These were the sounds of property owners, men who had struggled to save money and buy their own wagons and farm animals, their own land. Now, under one pretext or another, their farms were being taken away. The newly elected state officials claimed that these Negro farmers had not paid their back taxes; and since only officials had access to tax records, who could prove them mistaken? It had become a crime in the South to sell desirable property to a black man. And no freedman could afford to rent land at the prices charged the Negro. The high price of land was a trick to force the Negro to remain a sharecropper or laborer, working for the white man.

Then, in the wake of the clatter of the property owners, along those same trails flanking the great river, came another sound. This time it was the shuffle of thousands upon thousands of feet, an army adrift on the land, its simple belongings shoved into handkerchiefs or bulky cotton sacks. These were the families who

Harper's Weekly, October 21, 1876, caricatured the pressure often applied to make a Negro vote for the Democratic Ticket in the South.

Another woodcut from Harper's Weekly, October 19, 1872, shows the frequent result when a Negro could not be "persuaded" on how to vote.

had never owned property but who had dared claim their right to vote, and voted for the Reconstruction governments. The new White Leagues and the Ku Klux Klan complained that, when these men voted, too much money was spent on schools. The South could not afford such folly, they said.

Negro families like these were most often denied credit at the store, although no tenant family could live through the cotton-growing season without credit. Even when a man was granted credit, it was not unusual for his entire crop to be claimed by the store in repayment at the end of season. If a man could not read or write, how could he prove a storekeeper's books wrong?

For every one of these displaced people, heading north was a bold move. It is not easy to leave home. But hope for the future of their children drove them forward. Before leaving home many had dictated or written letters to the Governor of Kansas.

"Can we be free?"

"Can we have work and can we have our rights in Kansas?"

"Can our children go to school?"

In Washington, the Senate of the United States was amazed at reports of this sudden migration of thousands of people. It sent a committee south to investigate. Nearly seventeen hundred pages were filled with the testimony that the committee collected. Northern papers shocked their readers by publishing, for the first time, long accounts of what had been happening in the southern states. And Congress talked and debated. But despite the newspaper stories and the reaction of the public, Washington did nothing to protect the freedmen who remained behind in the former Confederate states.

Before the end of 1879, sixty thousand freedmen had made the long trip north to John Brown's state. From Point Coupee, Ouachita, Tensas, Franklin, Concordia, Madison, Nossier, and Caddo parish in Louisiana they came. From Meridian, Clinton,

Many southern emigrants were sheltered in St. Louis's Floral Hall when they first came up the Mississippi. These scenes are from Harper's Weekly, *July 5, 1879.*

Yazoo, Vicksburg, De Kalb, Pike, and Amite counties in Mississippi. From the states of Alabama and Arkansas. Some were nine weeks on the road from Texas, little steers no larger than calves trotting in front of the great horned oxen that dragged their wagons.

Most of the sixty thousand arrived in the spring of 1879. In February, a boat crowded with hungry men, women, and children docked in St. Louis. They were dressed for the cotton fields, and their bare feet left deep prints in the snow covering the piers. They had barely waited for the weather to warm up down South, before leaving Mississippi. They had wanted to be sure to reach Kansas in time for spring planting. They knew nothing about snow and cold.

That year, spring came even later than usual to Kansas. Many of the new arrivals fell sick and died. A few turned back. But more kept coming.

Kansas needed workers and farmers. The Governor made a speech in the Topeka Opera House, throwing wide in welcome the doors of John Brown's state and inviting freedmen to the broad acres of Kansas.

Sojourner's old friends from the antislavery days and woman's rights struggle began to bump into one another as volunteers arrived to help the freedmen get settled. In early May, a Kansas Freedmen's Relief Association was set up. Its agents scoured the state to find employment for the newcomers and to settle them in colonies on the land. From all over the country people sent contributions of money, food, and clothing, and from England came money to buy stoves, ox teams, seed, and more clothing.

To Sojourner Truth, this great movement of freedmen out of the South to Kansas truly seemed the work of her Lord. The task to which he had appointed her, she decided, had proven far too big for an old woman to accomplish alone. But the Lord had not forgotten her. When she had tired and stopped to rest, he had kept his own shoulder to the wheel and finished up the work.

Now she had one last long trip to make. Late in 1879, Sojourner picked up her box of "shadows" and headed west from Battle Creek. To pay her way she would stop and hold meetings as she traveled toward Kansas. There she expected to meet her friend Laura Haviland. They both had work to do.

Before she died Sojourner Truth had to make certain her people were properly settled on the land. She did not want to risk their ending up in the misery she had seen them endure in Washington. As she set out from Battle Creek, she told a reporter, "There will be, child, a great glory come out of that. I don't expect I will live to see it. But before this generation has passed away, there will be a grand change. This colored people is going to be a people. Do you think God has had them robbed and scourged all the days of their life for nothing?"

In Kansas, she and Laura went about urging the Negro immigrants not to settle down in the cities, where they could only become day laborers or vagrants, but to take advantage of the Homestead Law and apply to the public land office for land of their own.

Into the Light

THIRTY ONE

&✍ Sojourner Truth died at her home in Battle Creek, on November 26, 1883. When she died, she was not alone. Slowly, over the years, she had collected around her all the living members of her family. Diana, Elizabeth, and Sophie lived in Battle Creek now, with their husbands and children. To them she was mother or grandmother. But to the larger world, Sojourner Truth had become a legend.

Her friends were proud of the legend and encouraged it to grow. They claimed she died not at eighty-six but at one hundred and five—and this was difficult to contradict since no one could prove the birth date of a slave. Her friends, confusing her story with that of her parents, said she had had thirteen children and two husbands sold away from her. They insisted she had suckled the children of her white master, although this was never a custom in New York State as it had been in the plantation South. They said she was part Mohawk, and perhaps she was. Her many friends in Battle Creek were especially proud of the town's "first

One of the last-known photographs of Sojourner Truth.

COURTESY SCHOMBURG
COLLECTION, NEW YORK
PUBLIC LIBRARY

national figure." Yet probably not more than one Negro person in ten living in the United States during her lifetime even knew the name Sojourner Truth. In part, this could be explained by the fact that her activity was confined almost entirely to the North.

By the time Sojourner Truth died, forty years had passed since the day a servant known as Isabelle had set forth from Mrs. Whiting's house on Canal Street to do the work of her Lord. The work she had set out to do that day still lay around her, unfinished. The work of the Lord was never done. In fact, it must have seemed to the old fighter, as she lay dying on her couch at 10 College Street, that the work of the Lord was being rapidly *un-done*—that the world, even as she lay there, was moving backward.

The year of Sammy's death, Congress had at last passed a watered-down version of that bill outlawing discrimination for which Charles Sumner had so long struggled. For a few years— on paper, at least—there was a law that made discrimination against any American unlawful. But in 1883, the Supreme Court pronounced that piece of paper unconstitutional.

So many other tasks that she had set out to do were equally unfinished. At the Woman's Rights Convention in New York in 1867, Sojourner had warned, "If you want me to get out of the world, you had better get the women voting soon. I shan't go 'til I can do that." Yet, despite all the talking and lecturing, only a few states had granted women the right to vote.

Her death surprised no one. All year her health had been failing. The painful leg ulcers that had interrupted her work after Sammy's death returned again. The last three months of her life were months of great pain, but her mind remained clear and serene to the end. Once, long before, a friend had asked, "But, Sojourner, suppose there is no heaven. What will you say if you never get there?"

"What will I say if I don't get there?" she replied. "Why, I'll say 'Bless the Lord! I had a good time thinking I would.'"

Toward the last, Frances Titus called to see her and found Sojourner's eyes as radiant as ever. In a low voice that made no attempt to soar over the heads of an audience, the old woman sang her favorite hymn:

> *It was early in the morning,*
> *It was early in the morning,*
> *Just at the break of day,*
> *When he rose, when he rose,*
> *And went to heaven on a cloud.*

They buried Sojourner Truth in Oak Hill Cemetery, in Battle Creek, on a beautiful, clear November day. Many old friends had died before her. But Frederick Douglass sent a message from Washington and Wendell Phillips, in Boston, grieved at his old friend's passing. Some of Battle Creek's most prominent citizens acted as pallbearers, while more than one thousand people filed past the open casket.

The long, gaunt body of Sojourner Truth lay draped in black nun's veiling. She still wore the familiar white Quaker cap, however, and the white kerchief lay folded across her breast. Among the gifts leaning against the casket was a sheaf of ripened grain from Kansas.

"This short November day, now drawing to its close, was the perfect day of the season," wrote a reporter. "The long line of carriages, the hearse with its black plumes, the people—all so motionless—the cloudless sky, the great round, red sun lying low in the horizon. . . ." As the coffin was lowered into the ground, the sun sank slowly out of sight. Only a purple glow lingered, painting the hills and treetops of the town.

Many years earlier, in speaking of death, Sojourner Truth had compared it to stepping out of one room into another, "stepping out into the light."

"Oh," she had said, on that occasion, "Won't that be glorious!"

Today, people come from all over the country to see the grave in Oak Hill Cemetery. It is not hard to find. A six-foot white stone shaft rises toward the sky, flanked by slender green cypresses. On the back, carved letters form a cross: IN MEMORIAM SO-JOURNER TRUTH. On the front is the legend:

BORN A SLAVE IN ULSTER COUNTY,
STATE OF NEW YORK, IN 18TH CENTURY.
DIED IN BATTLE CREEK, MICHIGAN,
NOVEMBER 26, 1883. AGED ABOUT 105 YEARS.
"IS GOD DEAD?"

Around that carved shaft, under small unmarked stones, her family lies gathered—in death as in life in the shadow of Sojourner Truth.

A Selected Bibliography

The principal source for any life of Sojourner Truth is her own autobiography, the *Narrative of Sojourner Truth* as taken down by Olive Gilbert (Boston, 1850), particularly the final edition (Battle Creek, 1884) with materials added by Frances Titus and including Harriet Beecher Stowe's "The Libyan Sibyl." Other firsthand accounts are found in the *Reminiscences* of Lucy N. Colman (Buffalo, 1891); *Jewels in Ebony* by Fred Tomkins (London, 186?); *The History of Woman Suffrage* (3 vol.) by Susan B. Anthony, Elizabeth Cady Stanton, and Frances Gage (Rochester, 1887); "What I Found at the Northampton Association" by Frederick Douglass in Charles A. Sheffeld's *A History of*

Florence, Massachusetts (Florence, 1894); and in Gilbert Vale's account of the Matthias affair: *Fanaticism, Its Source and Influence* (New York, 1835).

Additional details based on original research are found in Berenice Lowe's "Michigan Days of Sojourner Truth" in the *New York Folklore Quarterly*, Summer, 1955; "The Family of Sojourner Truth," *Michigan Heritage*, Summer, 1962; and in materials presented by Mrs. Lowe to the Michigan Historical Collections of the University of Michigan and available on microfilm.

Full-scale recent biographies are Arthur H. Fauset's *Sojourner Truth: God's Faithful Pilgrim* (Chapel Hill, 1938) and Hertha Pauli's *Her Name Was Sojourner Truth* (New York, 1962). Mrs. Pauli's bibliography proved especially helpful to me.

For the social setting in which Sojourner spent the first 43 years of her life, an excellent general historical framework is given in *A Short History of New York State* by D.M. Ellis, J.A. Frost, H.C. Syrett, and H.J. Carman (Ithaca, 1957). More specific materials on life in Ulster County are in A.T. Clearwater's *History of Ulster County, New York* (Kingston, 1907); the chapter on Ulster in *Southeastern New York*, Vol. I, L.H. Zimm, ed. (New York, 1946); *History of Ulster County, New York*, N.B. Sylvester (Philadelphia, 1880); *History of New Paltz, New York, and its Old Families, 1678–1820*, Ralph LeFevre (Albany, 1903); and various issues of *Olde Ulster* (Kingston, 1905–14).

Additional information on slave and rural agricultural life can be found in *The Dutch and Quaker Colonies*, 2 vol., John Fiske (Boston, 1903); *Landlords and Farmers in the Hudson-Mohawk Region, 1790–1850*, D.M. Ellis (Ithaca, 1946); *History of Agriculture in the State of New York*, Ulysses P. Hedrick (Albany, 1933); *Sketches of Eighteenth-Century America*, St. Jean de Crevecoeur (repr. New Haven, 1925); *Reminiscences of Otsego County, New York*, Levi Beardsley (New York, 1852); *Life of*

Catherine Schuyler, Mary Gay Humphreys (New York, 1897); *Memoirs of an American Lady*, Anne Grant (London, 1808); *The Social History of Flatbush*, Gertrude Lefferts Vanderbilt (New York, 1881); "Social Aspects of the Slave in New York," Edward Olson, *Journal of Negro History*, (January 1941); and *Brooklyn and Long Island*, Scrapbook No. 60 in collections of Long Island Historical Society (Brooklyn).

David M. Schneider's *History of Public Welfare in New York State, 1609–1866* (Chicago, 1938) is good for descriptions of the living conditions of the poor and the ex-slaves. Volume 5 in the ten-volume *History of the State of New York*, edited by Alexander C. Flick (New York, 1933–37), is excellent on transportation. The steps that led to the abolition of slavery are authoritatively set forth in "Slavery in New York" by A.J. Northrup, *State Library Bulletin, History #4* (Albany, 1900); while "Federal Officeholders in New York State as Slaveholders, 1789–1805" by A.J. Alexander, *Journal of Negro History* (July, 1943), offers additional sidelights.

The condition of the Negro in New York City, during the years that Sojourner lived there and afterward, is documented in the *Negro at Work in New York City*, G.E. Haynes (New York, 1912); *Mirror for Gotham*, Bayrd Still (New York, 1955); *North of Slavery, The Negro in the Free States, 1790–1860*, Leon Litwack (Chicago, 1961); *Early Negro Church Life in New York*, G.W. Hodges (c. 1945, Layman Series, No. 1); *The Great Riots of New York, 1712–1873*, J.T. Headley (New York, 1873); *Immigrant Life in New York City, 1825–63*, Robert Ernst (New York, 1949); *Gangs of New York*, Herbert Asbury (New York, 1928); *New York: A Guide to the Empire State*, Federal Writers' Project, Work Projects Administration (New York, 1940); *The Cries of New York*, Samuel Wood (New York, 1822); and in the *Journal of Negro History*, "New York and the Negro, from 1783–1865," Leo H. Hirsch (October 1931), and "Economic Condition of Negroes of New York Prior to 1861," A.G. Lindsay (April, 1921).

Details on camp meetings and the revivalist movement were found in *Camp Meetings: Their Origins, History and Utility*, S.C. Swallow (New York, 1879); *They Gathered at the River*, Bernard A. Weisberger (Boston, 1958); and the *Bulletin of the Folksong Society of the Northeast*, No. 9 (Cambridge, Mass., 1930–37).

The history of the Northampton Association is described in Sheffeld (*op. cit.*) and Alice Eaton McBee's thesis "From Utopia to Florence" (Smith College, 1947).

For the abolitionist and Woman's Rights movements, most useful were Anthony, Gage, and Stanton (*op. cit.*); *Massachusetts in the Woman Suffrage Movement*, Harriet Jane Robinson (Boston, 1881); *Angels and Amazons*, Inez Haynes Irwin (Garden City, 1933); the 1850–51 issues of *The Liberator*, the weekly paper edited by William Lloyd Garrison; *American Chivalry*, Lillie Buffum Chase Wyman (Boston, 1913); *The Crusade Against Slavery*, Louis Filler (New York, 1960); and Henrietta Buckmaster's invaluable *Let My People Go* (New York, 1941).

In following Sojourner westward, I found the following very helpful: *History of Rochester and Monroe County, New York*, William F. Peck (New York, 1908); *Rochester, A Story Historical*, Jenny Marsh Parker (Rochester, 1884); *Early Religious History of Rochester*, Orlo J. Price (Rochester Historical Publications, Vol. III); *Life and Times of Frederick Douglass* by Frederick Douglass; Mrs. Colman's *Reminiscences* (*cf.* above); *Negro Americans in Ohio*, Charles H. Wesley (n.p. 1953); *Indiana: A Guide to the Hoosier State*, Federal Writers' Project (New York, 1947); *Michigan: A Guide to the Wolverine State*, ibid. (New York, 1941); and finally, *Battle Creek: Its Yesterday*, H.M. Stegman (Battle Creek, 1931).

Such periodicals as the *National Anti-Slavery Standard* and *Harper's Illustrated Weekly* were excellent for the events of the Civil War years. A first-rate account of the history of the Negro in Washington is in the Federal Writers' Project's *Washington: City and Capital* (Washington, 1937). Background on work among the freedmen is in *A Woman's Life Work*, Laura S. Haviland (Grand Rapids, 1881); "Aunt Laura—The Story of Laura Haviland" by Lillian M. Miller, *Northwest Ohio Quarterly*, Autumn, 1952; *Half a Century*, Jane G. Swisshelm (Chicago, 1880); *Crusader and Feminist: Letters of Jane G. Swisshelm, 1858–65*, ed. by A.J. Larsen (St. Paul, 1934); *Stories of Hospital and Camp*, Charlotte Elizabeth McKay (Philadelphia, 1876); *A History of the Freedmen's Bureau*, George R. Bently (Philadelphia, 1955); *Woman's Work in the Civil War*, L.P. Brockett (Philadelphia, 1867); *Negro Labor in the United States, 1850–1925*, Charles H. Wesley (New York, 1927); and *Reveille in Washington*, Margaret Leech (New York, 1941).

The Reconstruction and post-Civil War periods are well-described in *The Negro in the United States*, E. Franklin Frazier (New York, 1957). For the Negro exodus, I relied on George Williams' *History of the Negro Race from 1619 to 1880* (New York, 1883); Carter Woodson's *A Century of Negro Migration* (Washington, 1918); "The Exodus of 1879," by John Van Deusen in the *Journal of Negro History* (April, 1936); and *Negro Exodus: Report on Colored Immigrants in Kansas*, Colonel Frank H. Fletcher (188?).

Finally, the vain search for songs Sojourner might have sung as a slave in New York State led from the New York folksong anthologies of Harold W. Thompson to *The Negro and his Music* by Alain LeRoy Locke (Washington, 1936); to Miles Mark Fisher's *Negro Slave Songs in the United States* (London, 1953); and finally and most useful, to W.E.B. DuBois' *Souls of Black Folk* (New York, 1953).

Sojourner Truth Bibliography Since 1967

*Compiled by Nell Irvin Painter with the assistance of
Jean Fagan Yellin*

American Heritage. "Ain't I a Woman?" (August 1976).
Campbell, Karlyn Kohrs. "Style and Content in the
Rhetoric of Early Afro-American Feminists." *Quarterly
Journal of Speech.* (November 1986).
Collins, Helen and Bruce Bliven. *A Mirror for Greatness: Six
Americans.* New York: 1975.
Collins, Kathleen. "Shadow and Substance: Sojourner
Truth." *History of Photography.* (July–September 1983).
Fleming, John E. "Slavery, Civil War and Reconstruction: A
Study of Black Women in Microcosm." *Negro History
Bulletin* 38.6 (1975).

Lebedun, Jean. "Harriet Beecher Stowe's Interest in Sojourner Truth, Black Feminist." *American Literature* 46.3 (1974).

Loewenberg, Bert and Ruth Bogin, eds. *Black Women in 19th Century American Life: Their Words, Their Thoughts, Their Feelings.* University Park: 1977.

Mabee, Carleton, "Sojourner Truth, Bold Prophet: Why Did She Never Learn to Read?" *New York History* (January 1988).

——, "Sojourner Truth Fights Dependence on Government: Moves Freed Slaves Off Welfare in Washington to Jobs in Upstate New York." *Afro-Americans in New York Life and History* 14.1 (January 1990).

McDade, Thomas M. "Matthias, Prophet Without Honor." *New York Historical Society Quarterly* 62.4 (1978).

Ortiz, Victoria, *Sojourner Truth, A Self-Made Woman.* New York: 1974.

Painter, Nell Irvin. "Sojourner Truth in Life and Memory: Writing the Biography of an American Exotic." *Gender and History* 2.1 (Spring 1990).

——, "Sojourner Truth in Anti-Slavery: The Use and Limitation of a Prophetic Persona." In *An Untrodden Path: Antislavery and Women's Political Culture,* edited by Jean Fagan Yellin and John C. Van Horne. Forthcoming.

Porter, Dorothy. "Sojourner Truth Calls upon the President: An 1864 Letter." *Massachusetts Review* 13.1/2 (1972).

Shafer, Elizabeth. "Sojourner Truth: A Self-Made Woman." *American History Illustrated* 8.9 (1974).

Smith, Grace Ferguson. "Sojourner Truth: Listener to the Voice." *Negro History Bulletin* (March 1973).

Sterling, Dorothy. *Speak Out in Thunder Tones: Letters and Other Writings by Black Northerners, 1787–1865.* Garden City, NY: 1973.

Terry, Esther. "Sojourner Truth: The Person Behind the Libyan Sibyl." *Massachusetts Review* (Summer–Autumn 1985).

Yellin, Jean Fagan. *Women and Sisters: The Antislavery Feminists in American Culture.* New Haven: 1989.

Index

Journey Toward Freedom

The Story of Sojourner Truth